Baedeker's

AA

Loire

THE AUTOMOBILE ASSOCIATION

Imprint

Cover picture: Azay-le-Rideau, the Château

85 colour photographs
7 town plans, 6 sketches and diagrams, 5 special plans, 2 ground plans, 3 general maps, 1 road map

Text: Peter M. Nahm, Ostfildern

Editorial work: Baedeker Stuttgart

English Language: Alec Court

General direction: Dr Peter Baumgarten, Baedeker Stuttgart

English translation: James Hogarth

Cartography:
Ingenieurbüro für Kartographie Huber & Oberländer, Munich
Mairs Geographischer Verlag GmbH & Co.
Ostfildern-Kemnat (area map p. 160, road map)

Source of illustrations:
Baedeker (3), Goélette (1), Historia-Photo (6), Nahm (72), Pfänder (3)

Following the tradition established by Karl Baedeker in 1844, sights of particular interest and hotels of particular quality are distinguished by either one or two asterisks.

Only a selection of hotels and restaurants can be given: no reflection is implied, therefore, on establishments not included.

In a time of rapid change it is difficult to ensure that all the information given is entirely accurate and up to date, and the possibility of error can never be entirely eliminated. Although the publishers can accept no responsibility for inaccuracies and omissions, they are always grateful for corrections and suggestions for improvement.

2nd edition

© 1984 Baedeker Stuttgart
Original German edition

© 1985 Jarrold and Sons Ltd
English language edition worldwide

© The Automobile Association, 1985
United Kingdom and Ireland 57600

Licensed user:
Mairs Geographischer Verlag GmbH & Co., Ostfildern-Kemnat bei Stuttgart

Reproductions:
Gölz Repro-Service GmbH, Ludwigsburg

The name *Baedeker* is a registered trademark

Printed in Great Britain by Jarrold and Sons Ltd, Norwich

ISBN 0 86145 279 8

Contents

Preface

This pocket guide to the Loire is one of the new generation of Baedeker guides.

Baedeker pocket guides, illustrated throughout in colour, are designed to meet the needs of the modern traveller. They are quick and easy to consult, with the principal features of interest described in alphabetical order and practical details about location, opening times, etc., shown in the margin.

The present guide is divided into three main parts. The first part gives a general account of the Loire, its climate and economy, notable personalities associated with the river, its history and its art and architecture, together with suggested routes. The second part presents information about the towns, châteaux, etc., along the river, indicating their features of interest. The third part is devoted to practical information. Both the sights and the practical information are listed in alphabetical order.

The Baedeker pocket guides are noted for their concentration on essentials and their convenience of use. They contain numerous specially drawn plans and coloured illustrations; and an integral part of this guide to the Loire is a detailed road map covering the major part of the river's course.

Facts and Figures

General

The Loire is France's longest river, with a total course of 1020 km (635 miles). Together with its tributaries it drains an area of 120,000 sq. km (46,350 sq. miles), or some 22% of the total territory of continental France.

Course of the river

The source of the Loire lies in the northern Cévennes, which here form not only the watershed but also a climatic barrier between the Atlantic and the Mediterranean. The river then flows N through the hilly country of Velay into the Le Puy basin and the mining and industrial region of St-Etienne and Roanne, and continues in a wide curve between the old provinces of Bourbonnais and Nivernais towards its most northerly point, which it reaches at Orléans, at the S end of the Paris basin. From here it flows W, flanked by extensive water meadows, through the Massif Armoricain to reach the Atlantic at the southernmost point of Brittany.

The Loire has remained free from artificial regulation by man, apart from a few dams in its upper reaches near Le Puy and the extensive works of embankment – begun as early as the 12th c. – in the flatter parts of its course which is marked by numerous sandbanks and low tree-covered islands, the form of which is constantly changing owing to the considerable deposits of sediment brought down by the river. The absence of artificial regulation means that there are great variations in water level, and this may lead, particularly in spring, to the flooding of large areas of land along the river.

In consequence of this the shipping traffic on the river, once very considerable, declined when vessels of greater draught came into use and were unable to compete with the railways which took over the carriage of freight in the 19th c. Nowadays only the lowest part of the Loire, downstream from Nantes, is used by shipping; and ocean-going vessels must put in at the outer harbour of St-Nazaire on the Atlantic coast.

Canals

In modern times efforts have been made to overcome the problems of navigation on the Loire by the construction of canals, including the Canal de Roanne à Digoin (56 km – 35 miles) and the Canal Latéral à la Loire (196 km – 122 miles) from Digoin to Briare. From these there are branch canals providing links with other rivers – from Digoin the Canal du Centre (114 km – 71 miles) to the Saône, from Decize the Canal du Nivernais (174 km – 108 miles) to the Yonne, from Briare the Canal de Briare (56 km – 35 miles) to the Loing. There are interesting bridge-aqueducts at Digoin and Briare carrying the canals over the Loire. The canals are now increasingly used by pleasure craft, though there is still some commercial traffic.

◄ *Water meadows on the Loire near Vouvray*

Climate

Typical canal scenery

Tributaries

The principal tributaries flowing into the Loire from the S also draw their water from the wide expanses of the Massif Central. The largest left-bank tributaries are the Allier, the Cher, the Indre and the Vienne.

The Maine, which flows into the Loire from the N, is formed by the junction of the Mayenne and the Sarthe, which at this point is reinforced by the Loire.

Climate

Central France lies mainly in the zone of northern temperate climate, and thus in a region of predominantly W winds, in which the weather shows a more or less regular alternation throughout the year between depressions and areas of high pressure. Since the region lies in the W of the European continent the continental features in the climate give way before the moderating influence of the sea.

Temperatures

The range of temperature between the hottest and coldest months in the year is less than in Central Europe. The number of days of frost falls from E to W of the region. The average annual temperature is higher than in Central Europe, and the growing period lasts longer; it begins early, but largely loses its lead over Central Europe in the course of the summer.

Rainfall

Rainfall is distributed over the year, but whereas in Central Europe the maximum is reached in summer, in France – particularly nearer the coast – it occurs in autumn. There is, however, sufficient rain throughout the year. In the E there is a much more marked alternation between days with rain and days without rain, and in summer much of the total rainfall is accounted for by heavy thunder showers; in the W the rain tends to take the form of drizzle and rainy days are numerous, but on the coast the rain rarely lasts all day. At heights of over 1000 m (3300 ft) in the Massif Central, in spite of the relative nearness of the sea, there is often continuous snow cover into the month of May which may hinder the movement of traffic.

Economy

With a population density of some 90 inhabitants to the sq. kilometre (233 to the sq. mile), France is much more thinly settled than the United Kingdom. Accordingly agriculture plays a major part in the economy, some 60% of the country's area being devoted to arable farming and stock rearing.

Agriculture

France
—— boundaries of regions
⋯⋯ boundaries of départements

The Loire traverses the whole of central France

Economy

In Sologne, Poitou and the wooded regions on the upper course of the Loire forestry is also important. Agriculture yields vegetables, fruit and wine, and large expanses of land around Orléans are devoted to cereal growing. In Touraine and Anjou much wine is produced, including sparkling wine. In this area, too, there is an active mushroom-growing industry, carried on in extensive systems of tunnels and galleries hewn from the local tufa (often open to visitors).

In stock farming the famous white Charolais cattle predominate as producers of beef, the main areas of production being around Paray-le-Monial. In many areas, too, dairy farming and the production of cheese is practised (in the Sancerre region mainly goat's-milk cheeses).

Shellfish culture

On the coast, in the extensive mud-flats which are exposed at low tide, mussels and oysters are cultivated. In France oysters are not an expensive delicacy but a standard item in the diet. The coastal fisheries also make a contribution to the economy.

Industry

The largest industrial centres are in the Loire coalfield around Roanne and St-Etienne. The main industries are engineering and motor vehicle construction, textiles, glass and ceramics.

Energy supply

The Loire plays an important part in French energy supply. Given the circumstances of geography, the only hydroelectric power stations of any size are on the uppermost reaches of the river (e.g. at the Grangent dam, N of Le Puy); but the water of the Loire is used to cool the reactors in the nuclear power stations, at present six in number (some still under construction), which supply fully half France's output of atomic power.

Charolais cattle

Nuclear power station

Efforts are now being made to put the waste heat from the power stations to use, e.g. for the heating of glasshouses.

The Loire valley, particularly the area in Touraine and Anjou known as the "garden of France", possesses some of France's most popular tourist attractions in the form of the famous châteaux of the Loire. This is not only a region which attracts hundreds of thousands of foreign visitors but is also a favourite with French holidaymakers, who still outnumber tourists from other countries during the main holiday season.

Tourism

Notable Personalities

The great French novelist Honoré de Balzac, a native of Tours, began by studying law and later tried unsuccessfully to make a living in business, before achieving his first successes as a writer at the age of 30. An author of extraordinary productivity, his major work was the cycle of novels, begun in 1831 but never finished, which he called the "Comédie Humaine" – a realistic depiction, conceived on the grand scale, of French society between the Revolution and the "July Monarchy" of Louis-Philippe. His "Contes drolatiques" ("Ribald Tales") were also popular.

Honoré de Balzac (1799–1850)

The philosopher René Descartes – later known, in the humanist tradition, as Renatus Cartesius – was born at La Haye (now Descartes), in Touraine. After attending the Jesuit college at La Flèche he travelled about Europe, at first as a soldier, and later settled in Holland, where he lived for 20 years. The last year of his life was spent in Stockholm, whither he had been summoned by Queen Christina. He achieved fame with his philosophical system, the essence of which was the rational principle "cogito ergo sum" ("I think, therefore I am"). Descartes also did seminal work in mathematics, particularly geometry and algebra.

René Descartes (1596–1650)

In 1536 Diane de Poitiers became the favourite of King Henri II, husband of Catherine de Médicis. She enjoyed great political influence, but after the king's death was compelled by Catherine to leave the court and give up her much loved château of Chenonceau.

Diane de Poitiers (1499–1566)

François I, who came to the throne in 1515, belonged to a collateral line of the house of Valois. In 1514 he married Claude de France, daughter of Louis XII. In the Imperial election of 1519 he competed unsuccessfully against the Spanish Habsburg king Charles (who became the Emperor Charles V); and this rivalry later influenced his foreign policy, which was directed towards an understanding with the Pope and with other European countries favourable to the Reformation, in order to establish his own political constellation in opposition to the house of Habsburg. His domestic policy was designed to concentrate power in the king's hands, and thus foreshadowed the absolutism which was to give its name to a whole period of

François I (1494–1547)

Honoré de Balzac

François I

Catherine de Médicis

history. A patron of the arts and sciences, he attracted great artists and scholars to his court; and as a builder he left his mark both in the Loire valley and the Ile de France in the form of enlargements to older châteaux and the building of new ones.

Gregory of Tours
(538–594)

A scion of a noble Gallo-Roman family, Gregory is best known for his "History of the Franks". As bishop of Tours (from 573) he defended the position of the Church against secular rulers. He was later canonised.

Jeanne d'Arc
(c. 1410–1431)

Jeanne d'Arc, the "Maid of Orléans" and France's national heroine, was the daughter of peasants from the Vosges. Brought up in strict religious faith, she heard "voices" calling on her to free France from the English, who had been trying since 1339, in the Hundred Years War, to assert their claim to the French throne. She went to Chinon and Sully-sur-Loire and persuaded the Dauphin (Charles VII) to have himself crowned as king. Her most important military achievement was the raising of the English siege of Orléans (8 May 1429), which marked a turning-point in the war. Later she was taken prisoner by the Burgundians, who were allied with the English; whereupon she was tried by an ecclesiastical court and burned at the stake in Rouen on 30 May 1431. After her canonisation in 1920 she became France's second patron saint.

Catherine de Médicis
(1519–89)

Catherine de' Medici (de Médicis in French) was born in Florence, the daughter of Lorenzo II de' Medici, and was married to the future king Henri II at the age of 14. Her great rival was Diane de Poitiers, the king's influential favourite. After Henri's death she ruled as Regent for her son Charles IX. During the Wars of Religion she sought to stabilise the position of the kingdom between the Huguenots and Catholics. When the Calvinist Gaspard de Coligny, Admiral of France, tried to draw the young king on to the side of the Reformed faith Catherine caused thousands of Huguenots to be murdered in the St Bartholomew's Day massacre (24 August 1572).

Leonardo da Vinci
(1452–1519)

The great Italian artist, technician and scholar Leonardo da Vinci spent the last two years of his life at the court of King François I. Although there is no doubt that he was concerned in the design of a number of châteaux (e.g. Blois and

Chambord), it is not always possible to determine the exact extent of his contribution. The king presented him with the little château of Le Clos-Lucé, near Amboise, in which he died. He is buried in the chapel of the Château d'Amboise.

Louis XIV, the "Roi Soleil" ("Sun King"), was the very incarnation of the principle of absolutism ("L'état c'est moi" – "The state? I am the state"). In order to preserve the unity of France he revoked the Edict of Nantes in 1685 and took action to repress other strivings for religious reform. At the same time he defended the Gallican opposition to Papal supremacy. In spite of his political and military successes, however, he was unable to make good France's claim to hegemony in Europe.

Louis XIV
(1638–1715)

St Martin, one of the great Christian missionaries of the West and, as a hermit, the founder of important monasteries, became bishop of Tors in 371. After his death he was canonised and recognised as the Apostle of Gaul. He is best known for his action, while a soldier, in sharing his cloak with a beggar; his cloak was one of the royal treasures of the Frankish kingdom.

Martin of Tours
(c. 317–397)

Mary Queen of Scots was brought up in France and in 1558 married the Dauphin, who became François II in 1559. After his early death she returned to Scotland.

Mary Queen of Scots
(1542–87)

The doctor and scientist Denis Papin, born near Blois, is best known for his invention of a vessel for the production of high-pressure steam, with a safety valve (the "marmite de Papin", an ancester of the pressure-cooker and autoclave). He carried out many experiments with steam and compressed air and invented pumps, centrifuges and, it is said, a steam-propelled ship. A Huguenot, he was compelled by the revocation of the Edict of Nantes in 1685 to leave France, and after living for some time in Germany went to England and died there.

Denis Papin
(1647–1714)

Although Rabelais was a cleric, he is known to posterity as the author of rumbustious comic epics notable for their vigour of language and incident, mingling coarseness and humanist culture. Originally a Franciscan, he later joined the less severe Benedictine order, and finally became a secular priest and doctor. His best known work is the story of the giant Gargantua and his son Pantagruel, in several volumes, which is interpreted as a bitter satire on the manners of his time.

François Rabelais
(c. 1494–1553)

Maximilien de Béthune was a minister in the service of Henri IV and, as a Huguenot, a confidant of the king. When Henri came to the throne he made Béthune his financial adviser and charged him with the task of bringing order into the national economy and finances. His services were recognised by the title of Duc de Sully in 1606. After Henri's death Sully fell from power.

Duc de Sully
(Maximilien de Béthune,
1560–1641)

Charles Maurice de Talleyrand-Périgord, scion of an ancient and noble family, became bishop of Autun in 1788. As a member of the National Assembly he aligned himself in 1789 with the revolutionaries and became a leading representative of the Constitutional Church, taking the oath of allegiance to the Constitution in 1791. Thereupon he was threatened with excommunication by the Vatican and left the Church. After being condemned by the Convention as a royalist he lived in

Charles Maurice de
Talleyrand (1754–1838)

Notable Personalities

François Rabelais

Talleyrand

Jules Verne

America from 1794 to 1796. On his return he served the Directory and later Napoleon as foreign minister; but, rejecting Napoleon's great-power policies, he was dismissed in 1809. He represented France at the Congress of Vienna and was again appointed foreign minister by Louis XVIII.

Jules Verne
(1828–1905)

Jules Verne, a native of Nantes, was one of the first writers to exploit the great technological advances of the industrial age as a basis for what is now called science fiction. In recent years his work has been rediscovered, and it is astonishing with what precision he foresaw many scientific and technical developments.

François Villon
(François de Montcorbier,
1431–63)

The son of a poor family, François Villon was throughout his life a restless spirit. After taking his master's degree in Paris in 1452 he spent most of his time among rogues, vagabonds and adventurers and narrowly escaped execution in 1463. His poems ("Petit Testament", "Grand Testament"), cynical and brutally frank, provided a model for much later poetry by writers who had opted out of society.

History

Julius Caesar conquers the territory that is now France, then inhabited by a Celtic people, the Gauls.

58–51 B.C.

From about 250 the Franks begin to raid Gaul, and after 400 begin to settle there.

3rd–5th c. A.D.

Attila's Huns advance as far as Orléans, but are driven back by Bishop Aignan. Soon afterwards they suffer an annihilating defeat at the hands of the Romans and their auxiliaries in the battle of the Catalaunian Fields and withdraw to the east.

451

Orléans is taken by Clovis, king of the Franks.

498

Episcopate of Gregory of Tours. His "History of the Franks" is an important historical source on the development of the Merovingian kingdom.

573–593

Foundation of the Benedictine abbey of Fleury (now St-Benoît-sur-Loire).

7th c.

In a battle near Tours and Poitiers Charles Martel ("mayor of the palace" to the Merovingian king since 720) saves France by his victory over the Moors, who had thrust northward from Spain.

732

Charlemagne extends the Frankish kingdom and divides it up into counties.

768–814

The Carolingian Renaissance brings a great flowering of art and learning in the spirit of late antiquity. Among those who contribute to it is Théodulf, bishop of Orléans and abbot of St-Benoît.

8th–9th c.

Incursion by Norsemen into the Loire region. Charles III grants them possession of Normandy.

911

With the death of Louis V the French Carolingian line comes to an end. The throne passes to Hugues Capet, founder of the Capetian line.

987

Foundation of the abbey of Fontevraud.

1099

Henry Plantagenet becomes king of England as Henry II. He derives his claim from his mother, daughter of Henry I.

1154

The counties of Anjou and Touraine fall to the crown.

1204–05

The States General are summoned to meet for the first time.

1302

The States General condemn the order of Templars (established 1119), accused of heresy and immorality. All members of the order are arrested and many are put to death. At the Council of Vienne (1312) Pope Clement V dissolves the order.

1308–12

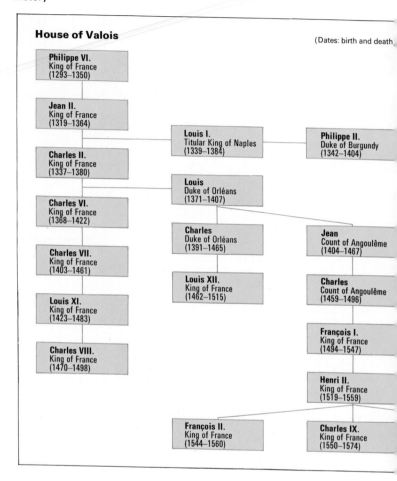

House of Valois

(Dates: birth and death)

Philippe VI.
King of France
(1293–1350)

Jean II.
King of France
(1319–1364)

Louis I.
Titular King of Naples
(1339–1384)

Philippe II.
Duke of Burgundy
(1342–1404)

Charles II.
King of France
(1337–1380)

Louis
Duke of Orléans
(1371–1407)

Charles VI.
King of France
(1368–1422)

Charles
Duke of Orléans
(1391–1465)

Jean
Count of Angoulême
(1404–1467)

Charles VII.
King of France
(1403–1461)

Louis XII.
King of France
(1462–1515)

Charles
Count of Angoulême
(1459–1496)

Louis XI.
King of France
(1423–1483)

François I.
King of France
(1494–1547)

Charles VIII.
King of France
(1470–1498)

Henri II.
King of France
(1519–1559)

François II.
King of France
(1544–1560)

Charles IX.
King of France
(1550–1574)

1328	With the death of Charles IV the main Capetian line becomes extinct. He is succeeded by Philippe VI, the first of the Valois kings.
1339–1453	Hundred Years War between France and England. Edward III of England claims the French throne on the basis of his descent from Isabelle, daughter of the Capetian Philippe IV, who had married Edward II. The English achieve major military successes, and in the battle of Maupertuis (1356) the Black Prince, Edward III's son, takes the French king Jean II prisoner. In spite of the treaty of Brétigny (1360) fighting resumes in 1369.

The Royal Line of France

House of Bourbon
(junior line)

The lily of the Bourbons

Charles I.
Duke of Vendôme
(1489–1537)

Antoine de Bourbon
King of Navarre
(1518–1562)

Louis I.
Prince de Condé
(1530–1569)

Henri IV.
King of France
(1553–1610)

Louis XIII.
King of France
(1601–1643)

Philippe I.
Duke of Orléans
(1660–1701)

Louis XIV.
King of France
(1638–1715)

Louis
"le Grand Dauphin"
(1682–1712)

Philippe
Duke of Anjou
(Philip V of Spain)

Louis XV.
King of France
(1710–1774)

Henri III.
King of France
(1551–1589)

Louis
Dauphin
(1729–1765)

In 1429 Jeanne d'Arc, a peasant girl from Lorraine, inspires the dispirited French army to new victories; she persuades Charles VII to have himself crowned at Reims as king of France; and on 8 May her forces relieve Orléans, under seige by the English. After her capture by the Burgundians, who are allied with the English, she is tried by an ecclesiastical court and on 30 May 1431 is burned at the stake in Rouen as a heretic.
By 1453 the English are driven out of France.

Duke René, known as the "Bon Roi René", reigns in Anjou. Although a luckless ruler, he is the greatest art patron of his day, and Angers becomes a famous artistic centre.

1434–71

19

1438	Charles VII signs the Pragmatic Sanction in Bourges. This gives the French Church a considerable degree of independence from Rome and marks the foundation of the Gallican movement.
1480	The fief of Anjou reverts to the crown and Louis XI incorporates it in the kingdom of France.
1494–1559	Italian campaigns: Charles VIII lays claim to Milan and Naples. He conquers these territories, but is unable to hold on to them. In 1513 his successor Louis XII is driven out of Italy by Swiss troops. François I recovers Milan. In 1519 he is an unsuccessful contender for the Imperial crown; and between 1521 and 1544 he wages four wars against the Emperor Charles V for predominance in Italy and possession of the Burgundian inheritance. In 1525 he is defeated and taken prisoner at Pavia and is compelled to renounce all claims to Italy.
	The Italian campaigns bring France into contact for the first time with the ideas of humanism and the Renaissance, which now spread from Italy into France and introduce a new era in both art and the humanities. Numbers of châteaux (Amboise, Chambord, Chenonceau, etc.) are built or rebuilt in the new Renaissance style.
1532	The union of Brittany with France is signed at Nantes.
1552	Treaty of Chambord: Henri II supports Maurice of Saxony's planned rising against the Emperor Charles V, receiving in return the three bishoprics of Metz, Toul and Verdun.
1560	Conspiracy of Amboise, an attempt by the Huguenots to obtain freedom to practise their religion. They seek to withdraw François II from the influence of the Catholic ducal house of Guise; but their plan miscarries, and thousands of them are executed.
1562–98	The Wars of Religion, in which France is riven by bloody fighting. Political as well as religious interests are involved. Hundreds of thousands of Huguenots flee from France.
1572	In the St Bartholomew's Day massacre (24 August) Catherine de Médicis, mother of the weak-willed Charles IX, causes the Huguenot leader Gaspard de Coligny and thousands of his followers to be killed.
1588	The Duc de Guise, leader of the Catholic League (established 1576), is murdered at Blois on Henri III's orders.
1593	In order to bring peace to the country Henri IV becomes a Catholic ("Paris is well worth a mass").
1598	The Edict of Nantes gives the Huguenots a limited degree of religious freedom. End of the Wars of Religion; strengthening of royal authority.
1604	Construction of the Canal de Briare, linking the Loire with the Seine.
from 1624	Under Cardinal Richelieu, followed by Cardinal Mazarin and Louis XIV, the crown reaches the summit of its power;

establishment of absolutism. Louis now makes Paris (the Louvre, and later Versailles) his main residence, and the Loire region loses its importance as the centre of French court life.

The great nobles and the courts oppose Mazarin's policies, and become involved in the risings known as the Fronde. Disagreements within the Fronde lead to its collapse. 1648–53

The French Revolution destroys the old feudal structures. Church property is confiscated, and many works of art are destroyed. There are mass executions at Nantes. 1789–95

Construction of the Canal Latéral à la Loire begins. 1822

Abd el-Kader, leader of Berber resistance to the French in Algeria, is interned in the Château d'Amboise. 1847–52

Franco-German War. Fighting at Orléans and elsewhere. 1870–71

Shipping on the Loire succumbs to the competition of the railways. c. 1900

First World War. In 1917 Tours becomes the headquarters of the American forces in France. Troops are landed at St-Nazaire. 1914–18

Second World War. In 1940 Tours is briefly the seat of the French government, forced by the German advance to leave Paris. Fierce fighting in Saumur. 1939–45

The first French atomic power station at Avoine-Chinon comes into operation. 1969

Foundation of the University of Tours. 1970

In order to control the flight of capital to other countries the French government imposes compulsory restrictions on foreign exchange and a temporary halt to increases in wages and prices. 1981

Signing of the Franco-German agreement on the relaxation of frontier controls. 1984

Frost damage causes the collapse of the Loire bridge at Sully. 1985

Kings of France, 987–1792

987– 996	Hugues Capet (b. *c*. 940)
996–1031	Robert II (b. *c*. 970)
1031–1060	Henri I (b. 1008)
1060–1108	Philippe I (b. 1052)
1108–1137	Louis VI (the Fat; b. *c*. 1081)
1137–1180	Louis VII (b. *c*. 1120)
1180–1223	Philippe II Auguste (b. 1165)
1223–1226	Louis VIII (b. 1187)
1226–1270	Louis IX (St Louis; b. 1214)
1270–1285	Philippe III (the Bold; b. 1245)
1285–1314	Philippe IV (the Fair; b. 1268)
1314–1316	Louis X (b. 1289)
1316–1322	Philippe V (b. 1293)
1322–1328	Charles IV (b. 1294)

Royal emblems

above, left:
Louis XII.

above, right:
François I.

below, left:
Anne de Bretagne

below, right:
Claude de France

1328–1350	Philippe VI (b. 1293)
1350–1364	Jean (the Good; b. 1319)
1364–1380	Charles V (the Wise; b. 1338)
1380–1422	Charles VI (b. 1368)
1422–1461	Charles VII (b. 1403)
1461–1483	Louis XI (b. 1423)
1483–1498	Charles VIII (b. 1470)
1498–1515	Louis XII (b. 1462)
1515–1547	François I (b. 1494)
1547–1559	Henri II (b. 1519)
1559–1560	François II (b. 1544)
1560–1574	Charles IX (b. 1550)
1574–1589	Henri III (b. 1551)
1589–1610	Henri IV (b. 1553)
1610–1643	Louis XIII (b. 1601)
1643–1715	Louis XIV (b. 1638)
1715–1774	Louis XV (b. 1710)
1774–1792	Louis XVI (b. 1754)

Art and Architecture

There are practically no remains of the prehistoric and early historical periods in the Loire valley, and few traces of Greek or Roman settlement.

In early Christian times religious houses were founded all over the region. Among them was the 7th c. abbey of Fleury (now St-Benoît-sur-Loire), with a scriptorium which, like that of Tours, enjoyed great reputation in the 8th c. These made their contribution to the Carolingian renaissance, which revived the spirit of Christian antiquity and was carried forward by the leading minds of the day.

Carolingian period

The architecture of the Carolingian period held to archaic forms, showing a preference for central plans. The church of St-Germigny-des-Prés (near St-Benoît-sur-Loire) is an example of this style.

The Romanesque style came to the fore about the year 1000. Its characteristic feature is the round-headed arch.

Romanesque

In religious architecture the basilican type became increasingly popular, and continued to predominate in the Gothic period. The basilica has a nave flanked by aisles, the nave being higher than the aisles; later a transept was added, and sometimes additional aisles. The interiors are of impressive effect in their ascetic bareness, but the capitals of pillars and columns are luxuriantly ornamented with plant motifs, animals and human figures. A specifically French feature is an ambulatory round the choir with radial chapels, as in the basilica (almost wholly demolished) of St Martin in Tours. Stylistic influences from Byzantine territory are relatively common, for example in the cathedral of Le Puy (12th c.).

Of great significance for the development of Romanesque church architecture was the Cluniac reform of the 10th and 11th c., which originated in the Benedictine abbey of Cluny in Burgundy. The transept is now given greater emphasis, producing a distinct cruciform plan, and a tower is built over the crossing, while a porch is added at the W end. Examples of this style are the churches of Paray-le-Monial, St-Benoît-sur-Loire and La Charité (this last only partly preserved). The cathedral of Nevers also goes back to Romanesque origins.

This period also saw a first flowering of stained glass. Good examples can be seen in Angers cathedral and the Trinité church in Vendôme.

A transition between Romanesque and Gothic is seen in the so-called "Plantagenet style" of Anjou and Touraine.

The Gothic style which began to establish itself in the 12th c. originated in France (Normandy), and is therefore sometimes called the "style français".

Gothic

While in Romanesque architecture the roof was still borne on massive walls, with few windows, in the Gothic period the introduction of ribbed vaulting made it possible to direct the lateral thrust of the vaulting into the foundations by way of the ribs and so relieve the walls, which could now be opened up by large areas of window.

This was the great age of stained glass (Bourges and Tours cathedrals). Churches become steadily larger; the cruciform plan is obscured or disappears altogether (e.g. Bourges cathedral). The proportions of the church now alter, with the emphasis on vertical lines. The narrow naves with their pointed vaulting direct the eye upwards. Doorways, windows and walls have rich tracery decoration, the characteristic feature in which, found in a variety of forms, is the foil (the small arc formed by the cusps of the tracery). There is a great flowering, too, of sculpture, for example in the figured doorways of churches.

Secular building also develops, and sturdy castles, handsome burghers' houses and large hospices or hospitals are erected.

In the later Gothic period the tracery becomes ever more elaborate, its intricacy of form almost becoming an end in itself. This gives rise eventually to the "Flamboyant" style, so called after the flame-like appearance of the ornament. Stone sculpture and wood-carving take on the delicacy of filigree work.

Book illumination plays an important part in Gothic art. Duc Jean de Berry and Louis d'Anjou employ Dutch and Flemish miniature painters (among whose masterpieces is the famous Book of Hours of the Duc de Berry). Jan Bandol (Hennequin de Bruges) designs the magnificent "apocalypse" tapestries.

Towards the end of the Gothic period the valley of the middle Loire, between Orléans and Saumur, began to develop into the favourite resort of the French kings. The first of them was Charles VII, who made Chinon his residence, and in the short space of 150 years (until the death of Henri III in 1589) a whole series of sumptuous châteaux were built.

Renaissance

On his Italian campaigns Charles VIII came into contact with the art of the Renaissance, which had developed in Italy from about 1420. Deeply impressed by this "rebirth" of antiquity, he had his ancestral castle enlarged in the new style, and Amboise thus became the starting-point of the triumphal progress of the Renaissance throughout the whole of France.

Among Charles's successors the most enthusiastic builder was François I, whose emblem, a salamander spitting fire, is to be seen in many châteaux. Among new châteaux built during this period were Châteaudun, Chenonceau, Blois and Chambord. Whereas in earlier times castles had been designed for military purposes and sited in accordance with strategic, tactical and other topographical requirements, the châteaux now built were conceived for splendour and for show, although their architectural form might still incorporate features reminiscent of the older defensive structures – massive corner towers, wall-walks with machicolations, moats. François I also attracted leading foreign artists to his court, among them Leonardo da Vinci. Church building now took second place to secular architecture, and stylistically stood apart from the new trends. One artistic genre which now came to the fore was tapestry. The large wall hangings, which served not only for decoration but also as a means of bringing some warmth to under-heated rooms, were mostly produced in Flanders, but manufactories were also established in France. It took a tapestry weaver a whole year to produce a single square metre of tapestry.

The French classical period coincided in time with the Baroque art which was now developing, mainly in Italy and Germany; but since classicism consciously and deliberately distanced itself from the vigorous style and sometimes overloaded ornament of Baroque and pursued its own independent development, always aiming at greater severity and formal discipline, it is fair to use this distinctive designation.

Essentially, too, the French classical period coincided with the age of absolutism. Since the king, and with him the nobility, increasingly preferred to live in or near Paris, building activity in the Loire valley now fell off sharply. As an example of classical architecture the Gaston d'Orléans wing in the Château de Blois may be cited.

The classical style continued into the late 18th c., and then gave place, in painting and sculpture, to the Romantic movement.

In architecture the classical style was followed by the style known as Historicism, which involved imitating various earlier styles. This had the effect of arousing interest in medieval architecture, but the restorations of medieval buildings which were now undertaken frequently resulted in distortion and falsification.

Few sculptors of the school known as Realism are still remembered, such as Pierre-Jean David d'Angers or Auguste Rodin and Aristide Maillol (neither of whom worked in the Loire valley); Maillol pointed the way forward to the 20th c.

19th c. painting developed from Romanticism to Realism, which was followed by Impressionism. The leading artists worked mainly in Paris or in the S of France.

From the turn of the 19th c. art and architecture became increasingly international. Art passed through a whole series of schools – Expressionism (the "Fauves"), Constructivism, Cubism and Surrealism (one example of which is a fountain in Amboise by Max Ernst, a German artist who lived for many years in France). The principal works of these schools can be seen in the great museums of France.

Notable modern engineering achievements are the bridge over the Loire at St-Nazaire and the bridge linking the island of Noirmoutier with the mainland.

Quotations

(Evidence in the proceedings for the rehabilitation of Jeanne d'Arc.)

"On that day we halted in the open country, and again on the next day. On the third day we came near to Orléans, where the English held the river bank with their fieldworks. The king's army moved so closely up to the positions of the English that Englishmen and Frenchmen could observe each other. The Loire then had so little water that the ships could neither sail upstream nor approach the enemy bank. Then the water rose, almost suddenly, so high that the ships could sail towards the army. Jeanne embarked on one of the ships along with a number of soldiers in order to enter the town. On her orders I went back to Blois with the priests and the banner, and a few days later returned with a strong body of men, passing unhindered through Beauce to Orléans, always at the head of the party with the priests and the banner . . .

"When Jeanne heard that we were approaching she came to meet us, and together we entered Orléans without hindrance, taking in food under the very eyes of the English. It was truly matter for wonder that the English, with all their power and might, allowed our small force of men loyal to the king to pass before their eyes. They saw and heard the priests singing, and I was among them carrying the banner . . .

"On Ascension day Jeanne called on the besiegers in a letter to surrender. 'I should have sent you my letter in a more proper way,' she wrote, 'but that you hold my heralds prisoner; you have as your prisoner my Guienne Herald. Send them back to me, and I will deliver up to you some of your men taken at Saint-Loup; those at any rate who are not already dead.'

"Then she took an arrow and tied the letter to its tip, and asked an archer to send it to the English, crying out, 'Read it! Here is news for you!' The English received the arrow and the letter and read it. Then they were heard crying out in anger, 'News from the whore of the Armagnacs!' When Jeanne heard this she began to sob and weep hot tears, and called on the King of Heaven for aid. On the day after Ascension, that is on Friday, I rose early and heard Jeanne's confession, and then I sang mass in her presence and that of the townsfolk of Orléans."

Wolfgang Koeppen
German writer
"Travels in France" (1961)

"Tours too – the ancient city, the home of Rabelais, Balzac and the young Descartes – seems to have lost for ever the patina of its great centuries in the recent destructions. The main street, the Rue Nationale, which runs through the town in a straight line from the Wilson Bridge on the Loire, has been rebuilt and is active and lively, but faceless. But first impressions are deceptive, and even a new square such as the Place du Maréchal-Foch is, at any rate in the evening, authentic France. The people of Tours sit outside the trim hotels and brightly lit cafés, and the trees have grown again, and again been trimmed. The liveliest scene, however, is in Place Jean-Jaurès – a popular forum, appropriately named after the people's friend, the martyr for peace. Tree-lined avenues, cafés, brasseries, tradesmen, commercial travellers, postmen, recruits, young people, mothers, swarms of children. They drink beer, they drink lemonade, but all of them eat at home. The restaurants offer meals, but they are bad, or both dear and bad. Delicious wine is produced in the countryside around Tours, but the restaurants and cafés get the wretched stuff they sell from factories. Still, I stayed in Tours; I saw the witches' square Place Plumereau, the Rue du Change, old houses from the time of Louis XI, weary and bent with age, but still lived in, still loved, still hated; the world of Rabelais, but still home. The smell of evening meals, children's voices behind half-closed shutters, the squadron of youths on motorcycles roaring round sharp corners. Lanes running down to the river, the width of a man's shoulders. Voices preparing for the night, hanging in the air like a choir of spirits. Over the Loire wind and clouds and the lightning of a distant thunderstorm."

"Towards the evening, when we drove from the road flanking the Loire through the park-like forest, the Château de Chambord, broad-based in its setting of meadowland, was already surrounded by a light haze. Only the tops of massive towers at each end of the château and the twin towers of the central range with its bewildering profusion of gables, chimneys and other structures on the roof terrace were still clear against the light. It looked unreal, with this closely packed huddle of roof structures, like so many organ-pipes; almost Oriental and, bathed in the evening light, almost like a fairytale castle. The jagged outline of the roof was reflected, too, in the lake which extended in front of the flowerbeds of the gardens, reaching far out into the apparently endless clearing.

"On the way there we had several times seen pheasants, reddish-gold apparitions suddenly raising their heads in the meadows bordering the forest. Here, where once had stood a modest hunting lodge, it was lonely enough for grazing red deer and roe deer, or fallow deer as they are depicted in old tapestries, which often show hunting scenes with courtiers, ladies and huntsmen blowing horns, noble in the manner of antiquity or of legend. For scenes of this kind would have been historically appropriate in front of this prospect of the château, with the undergrowth shrouded in the evening mist, while the sunny afterglow of the day still lingered on the tips of the trees."

Otto Rombach
German writer
"Back to France" (1973)

"Cinq-Mars, his glance fixed on the great window of the dining room, looked sadly out on the beautiful landscape in front of his eyes. The sun shone in full splendour, colouring in gold and emerald the bank of the Loire, the trees and the grass; the sky

Alfred de Vigny
French poet and writer
"Cinq-Mars" (1826)

Evening on the Loire

was purest azure, the water a shimmering yellow, the islands brilliant green. Beyond the rounded lines of the islands could be seen the large lateen sails of the cargo vessels, lying there like a fleet in ambush. 'O nature, nature!' he said to himself. 'Fair nature, farewell!'"

Suggested Routes

Time required

To follow the course of the Loire (1020 km – 634 miles) from its source to its mouth, taking in the principal places of interest within reach of the river – not counting the distance to the starting-point and the return from the finishing-point – may require a journey taking almost three weeks. The route goes through some of the finest scenery in France, leading as it does from the Massif Central and Auvergne around Burgundy and then through Touraine, Anjou and the extreme S of Brittany to the flat sandy coasts of the Vendée.

Visitors with less time at their disposal will require to confine themselves to the middle course of the Loire, starting perhaps from Orléans, which is only 134 km (83 miles) from Paris. This includes the stretch of greatest tourist interest and the most popular with visitors, between Blois and Angers. Most of the route runs through Touraine, long known as the "garden of France"; and in this area are the finest and best known of the châteaux.

For visitors coming from the E it may be convenient to join the route described below at Nevers. This involves a distance – again excluding the journey to the starting-point and from the finishing-point – of some 1200 km (750 miles).

Access

The source of the Loire, at the foot of the Gerbier de Jonc, can be conveniently reached from the Rhône valley (the A7 motorway, N7 or N86), branching W at Tournon, just N of Valence, and continuing on minor roads via Lamastre and Le Cheylard. Alternatively it is possible to cut through central France to Le Puy, from which it is a short distance SE to the Gerbier de Jonc.

Nevers can be reached from the N on N7 (from Paris). Orléans and the lower part of the Loire valley are reached from the N on the A10 motorway from Paris, or on one of the *routes nationales* passing to the W of Paris (perhaps via Beauvais or Chartres).

Route

In this description the names of places with a separate entry in the "A to Z" section of the guide are printed in **bold**.

From the **Gerbier de Jonc** the route follows the river through the **Loire Gorge** on roads which are sometimes narrow and winding, and comes to **Le Puy**, on the eastern border of the Auvergne.

Around **St-Etienne** extends the industrialised Loire basin, in which, farther N, is the town of **Roanne**. The route continues by way of **Paray-le-Monial** and **Moulins**, W of the river, to **Nevers**.

From **La Charité** it is worth making a detour to **Bourges**, returning to the river at **Sancerre** and continuing via **Gien**, **Sully** and **St-Benoît** to **Orléans**.

Beyond Orléans there is another rewarding excursion to **Châteaudun** and **Vendôme**, N of the river, returning E to rejoin it at **Beaugency**.

From **Blois** visits can be paid to the châteaux of **Chambord**, **Cour-Cheverny**, **Valençay** and **Loches**, situated on tributaries of the Loire. The route then continues via **Chenonceaux** to **Chaumont**, on the Loire, which is followed via **Amboise** to **Tours**.

At **Langeais** we cross to the S bank of the Loire to see **Villandry** and **Azay-le-Rideau**; then via **Ussé** to **Chinon**. After **Fontevraud-l'Abbaye** we return to the left bank of the Loire, which is followed to **Saumur**.

Farther downstream are the large towns of **Angers** and **Nantes**; and at **St-Nazaire** the Loire flows into the Atlantic. To the N of the estuary is the coastal resort of **La Baule**; to the S lies the offshore island of **Noirmoutier**.

A summary of the main places of interest along the course of the Loire from its source to its mouth can be found inside the back cover.

Cave dwellings near Saumur

Sights from A to Z

Within each entry the various features of interest are, so far as possible, arranged in a convenient order for sightseeing. Other places in the surrounding area are listed in alphabetical order at the end of the entry.

Amboise

Region: Centre
Département: Indre-et-Loire
Altitude: 60 m (197 ft)
Population: 11,000

The ancient little town of Amboise lies 25 km (15 miles) E of Tours on the left bank of the Loire, in the middle of which is the long narrow Ile St-Jean. To the S, between the Loire and the Cher, is a large expanse of forest.

Situation

At the beginning of the 12th c. Fulco Nerra, Count of Anjou, built a fortified castle here. On this spur of hill rising above the valley successive lords of Amboise created a powerful stronghold, parts of which were incorporated in the later château. When Louis d'Amboise fell into disfavour with Charles VII the town was confiscated by the crown (1434). The château was now considerably enlarged and sumptuously appointed to make it a worthy residence for the king.
Charles VIII, who was born in Amboise, set out in 1494 to conquer the kingdom of Naples. The attempt failed, but the king brought back from Italy a number of artists, who were mainly employed on the interior decoration of the château (which has not been preserved).
In 1560 the Huguenots, seeking in the Conspiracy of Amboise to secure freedom of worship, tried to withdraw King François II from the influence of the Dukes of Guise, who were bitterly opposed to the ideas of the Reformation. The plot was unsuccessful, and many Calvinists (said to number 1200) were hanged on the balcony of the château or drowned in the Loire.

History

*Château

The château as we see it today still shows Late Gothic features (Flamboyant style), but predominantly it is a Renaissance building, reflecting the style with which Charles VIII had become acquainted in Italy and which, starting from Amboise, was to spread throughout France. After Charles's accidental death building work was continued by his successors; and in 1517 François I summoned Leonardo da Vinci, the greatest artistic and technological genius of his day, to contribute to the work.

Location
Rue Victor-Hugo

Opening times
Daily 9 a.m.–noon and 2–6.30 p.m.

Conducted tours

Admission charge

◀ *Symbol of royal power: the Château de Chambord*

Château of Amboise, Chapelle St-Hubert

Son et lumière
See Practical Information

During the 19th c. the southern part of the château – then in private ownership – was demolished. What remained was restored in the time of the Third Republic (after 1870).

Exterior

On the N side of the château, facing the river, the substructure is formed by massive retaining walls. Above this is the richly articulated façade with its balcony fronted by a fine wrought-iron grille. To the left is a sturdy round tower, the Tour des Minimes, containing a ramp giving entry to the château for horses and carriages.

From the main road through Amboise (D751) Rue Victor-Hugo passes the approach to the château, which is entered by way of a covered passage through the walls on the SW side,

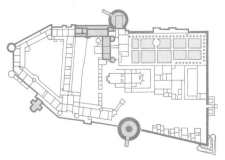

Amboise
Château

as it was in the 17th c.

1 Chapelle St-Hubert
2 Gothic wing
3 Renaissance wing
4 Tour des Minimes
5 Gardens
6 Chapel
7 Tour Hurtault

100 m

110 yd

directly below the Chapelle St-Hubert, at the entrance to which the access road comes to an end.

The Chapelle St-Hubert, on the ramparts of the château, was built about 1491 by Charles VIII and his wife Anne de Bretagne. Particularly fine is the Late Gothic doorway, with a relief depicting the legend of St Hubert. The tympanum of the doorway, with figures of the Virgin and the founders, dates from the 19th c., when the roof and ridge turret were renewed. In the left transept is the memorial of Leonardo da Vinci, who is buried here. The stained glass is modern.

Chapelle St-Hubert

On the N side of the terrace, at right angles to one another, are the two surviving wings of the Logis du Roi (King's Lodging). The wing parallel to the river is Gothic, the other one Renaissance. The difference between the two styles is particularly marked in the dormer windows (*lucarnes*).
Passing through the Salle des Gardes (Guard Room; two suits of armour, Aubusson tapestries, Gothic furniture), we come out on to the arcaded terrace (magnificent view of the Loire valley). On the rear wall of the loggia is a plan of the château as it was in the 16th c. Then, by way of the Tour des Minimes with its spiral ramp, we go up into the Renaissance wing (tapestries, Gothic and Renaissance furniture).
On the first floor of the Gothic wing, to which we now return, is the large Salle de Justice (Court Room), in which the Huguenots were condemned to death. They were hanged from the iron grille outside the hall, and it is said that François II and his young wife Mary Queen of Scots were present at this mass execution.

Logis du Roi

Chapelle St-Hubert, doorway

Figure, Max Ernst fountain

Amboise

Gardens

The gardens of the château lie to the E of the Logis du Roi. On the site of a chapel which was demolished in the 18th c. is a memorial to Leonardo da Vinci.
On the S side of the château rises the Tour Hurtault, which has a diameter of 24 m (79 ft) (3 m – 10 ft more than the Tour des Minimes).

Lower town

Hôtel de Ville

The old Hôtel de Ville (Town Hall), in the street running alongside the Loire, dates from the 16th c.; it now houses a small museum (manuscripts, pictures, etc.). Facing it is the church of St-Florentin (15th c.), with a Renaissance tower. A few paces S stands the Tour de l'Horloge (Clock Tower), a relic of a 15th c. town gate.

*Max Ernst Fountain

To the W of St-Florentin, on the Loire embankment, is the Fontaine d'Amboise, a monumental fountain by the German Surrealist Max Ernst (1891–1976), who lived for many years in France. This lighthearted work is popularly known as the *grenouille allemande*, the "German frog".

Church of St-Denis

In the SW of the town is the 12th c. church of St-Denis. Notable features of the interior are the fine Romanesque capitals, a 16th c. Entombment and (in the N aisle) a painting attributed to the Italian artist Primaticcio (1505–70).

Postal Museum

The Musée de la Poste (daily 9.30 a.m.–noon and 3–6 p.m.), in a 16th c. house in Rue Joyeuse, to the S of the Château, contains a wide range of exhibits, including uniforms, equipment, model vehicles, etc.

Le Clos-Lucé

Location
Rue Victor-Hugo

Opening times
Daily 9 a.m.–noon and 2–7 p.m.

Admission charge

The little château or manor house of Le Clos-Lucé, once the home of Leonardo da Vinci, lies to the SE of the Château d'Amboise in a small park. On the ground floor are a series of rooms furnished in 18th c. style. From the kitchen (fine exposed red brick walls) a staircase leads down to the basement, which houses a collection of models of machines made for the well known computer firm IBM on the basis of Leonardo's original designs. There was formerly an underground passage from the basement of Le Clos-Lucé to the Château d'Amboise, 500 m (550 yd) away.
On the first floor is the room in which Leonardo is said to have died in the arms of his royal patron. By the window (view of the Château d'Amboise) is a reproduction of a drawing by Leonardo showing the Château as it was in his day.

Pagode de Chanteloup

Location
3 km (2 miles) S

The Pagode de Chanteloup, a Chinese-style pagoda built in the late 18th c. stands to the S of the town in the Forêt d'Amboise, just to the right of the main road (D31). Standing 44 m (144 ft) high, it is the only surviving relic of a large Baroque château, built about 1715 and later considerably enlarged, which was sold to a contractor about 1800 and demolished for its stone.

Angers

Region: Pays de la Loire
Département: Maine-et-Loire
Altitude: 48 m (157 ft)
Population: 140,000

Angers, once capital of the county of Anjou and now chief town of the département of Maine-et-Loire, a university town and the see of a bishop, lies half-way between Tours and Nantes on both banks of the Maine, which flows into the Loire 8 km (5 miles) SW of the town.
A good bargain for visitors is an "all-in" ticket giving admission to the town's principal sights.

Situation

In Gallo-Roman times Angers was the chief town of the territory occupied by the Andecavi, a Gallic tribe. After taking the town the Romans built a fortress above the river. In the 9th c. the town was occupied by the Norsemen, but was soon recovered by Charles the Bald. With the rise of the Fulconids, viscounts and from some 950 counts of Anjou, the town and surrounding region of Anjou enjoyed a time of great prosperity, and numerous military and religious buildings were erected, particularly in the time of Fulco Nerra. Geoffroy V (1129–51) was the first to bear the name Plantagenet (after his heraldic plume, a stylised broom plant). His son Henry was the first Plantagenet to occupy the English throne, as Henry II. In the 12th c., therefore, Anjou became an English possession.

History

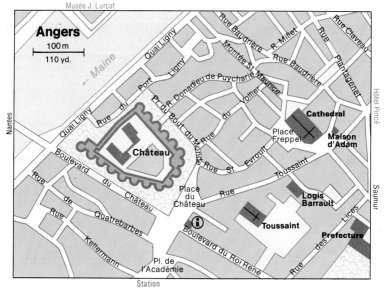

Porte des Champs

Maison d'Adam

Charles of Anjou was granted possession of the kingdom of Naples and the island of Sicily by the Pope, but his ambitious political plans were brought to naught by the Sicilian Vespers (1282), in which 6000 Frenchmen were killed by the Sicilians. Perhaps the best known figure in the history of Angers is René I, popularly called the "bon roi René". Although unsuccessful politically – losing Anjou's remaining territories in Italy – he was a cultivated and gifted patron of the arts who made his capital into a great artistic and cultural centre.

*Château

Location
Promenade du Bout-du-Monde

Opening times
Palm Sunday–15 June, daily
9.30–11.50 a.m. and
2–5.45 p.m.; 16–30 June,
daily 9.30–11.50 a.m. and
2–6 p.m.; 1 July–15 Sept.,
daily 9 a.m.–7 p.m.
16 Sept.–Palm Sunday, daily
9.30 a.m.–noon and
2–5.30 p.m.

Admission charge
(Covered by all-in ticket)

The château stands on an isolated rocky plateau rising 32 m (105 ft) above the left bank of the Maine, ringed by massive walls and 17 round towers which rise to heights of between 40 and 60 m (130 and 200 ft) above their bases. Originally erected by Fulco Nerra, the castle was rebuilt by Louis IX. During the Wars of Religion Henri II ordered the towers to be pulled down, but in the event only the helm roofs were destroyed.

Of the castle's two original entrances only the Porte de la Ville, on the N side, is still open. The other, the Porte des Champs, is half-way up the outer walls between the two towers at the south

After crossing the moat, which is partly laid out with flowerbeds and partly an enclosure for deer, visitors enter the spacious courtyard. To the right are the Chapel, the Logis Royal and the Logis du Gouverneur. The King's and Governor's Lodgings contain 15th and 16th c. tapestries.

Courtyard

In the passage below the little gatehouse in the centre of the courtyard, to the left, is the entrance to the modern building which houses the magnificent Tenture de l'Apocalypse, a series of 70 tapestries depicting the Revelation of St John. Made between 1375 and 1380, they were the work of the Paris tapestry weaver Nicolas Bataille, the designs being based on miniatures of the period. On the wall opposite the tapestries are reproductions of the scenes and the corresponding passages in the Book of Revelation. Explanatory text (in English as well as in French) can be borrowed at the entrance to the room. At the far end of the room, below floor level, are the excavated remains of a Romanesque chapel.

** "Apocalypse" tapestries

Beyond the gatehouse is an outlook terrace with a view of the river.

There are impressive panoramic views from the castle ramparts, particularly from the two highest towers. Visitors can walk round on considerable stretches of the walls.

Ramparts

The Apocalypse: The beast out of the earth brings down fire from heaven

*Cathédrale St-Maurice

Location
Place Freppel

To the E of the château, in the centre of the old town, is the Cathedral, which is approached from the Maine by a handsome ramp and staircase. Some of the figures on the well-preserved Gothic doorway have still traces of their original colouring. In the tympanum is a figure of Christ enthroned, surrounded by the symbols of the Evangelists, and above this are eight equestrian statues (16th c.) of the companions of St Maurice. The façade is crowned by three towers; the central tower was rebuilt in the High Renaissance period.

Treasury

A notable feature of the aisleless interior is the rich Treasury, in a room to the left (admission charge; included in all-in ticket), with gold and silver reliquaries and monstrances and an antique marble bath converted for use as a font.

*Stained glass

The beautiful stained glass, apart from the modern glass, dates from three different periods.
The high windows on the left-hand side of the nave, depicting scenes from the life of the Virgin and the martyrdoms of St Catherine of Alexandria and St Vincent, are 12th c. The massive carved pulpit on this side is 19th c. work. The two rose windows and the Pietà in the transept date from the 15th c. In the apse, behind the High Baroque altar (18th c.), are figures of saints and martyrs, between them a Tree of Jesse and scenes from the Passion. The stained-glass windows on the right-hand side of the nave are modern.
Also on the right-hand side of the nave is the dark Chapelle Notre-Dame-de-Pitié.

Maison d'Adam

Location
Place Ste-Croix

Immediately behind the apse of the Cathedral stands the Maison d'Adam, a handsome and well-preserved half-timbered house of the 15th–16th c. Particularly notable are the numerous figures carved on the vertical beams.

Logis Barrault

Location
Rue du Musée

Admission charge
(Covered by all-in ticket)

The Logis Barrault is a fine 15th c. burgher's mansion. It now houses the Musée des Beaux-Arts (Museum of Fine Art; summer 9 a.m.–noon and 2–6 p.m., winter 10 a.m.–noon and 2–4 p.m.), which contains the complete works (some originals but chiefly copies) of the sculptor Pierre-Jean David d'Angers (1788–1856), together with a picture gallery (mainly 17th and 18th c. works).

Eglise Toussaint

Close by is a little Gothic church, the Eglise Toussaint (All Saints), at present in course of restoration.

Hôtel Pincé

Location
Rue Lenepveu

Some 200 m (220 yd) N of the Cathedral is the Hôtel Pincé (built 1523–30), the finest private mansion in Angers. It is now occupied by the Musée Turpin de Crissé (daily 9 a.m.–noon and 2–6 p.m.): enamels, prints and graphic art, material from East Asia, Greek vases.

Admission charge
(Covered by all-in ticket)

Musée Jean Lurçat

This museum, housed in the 12th c. Hôpital St-Jean, displays tapestries by the painter Jean Lurçat (1892–1966), best known as the reviver of the art of tapestry. The large Gothic hall, originally a hospital ward, contains ten brilliantly colourful tapestries under the collective title of the "Chant du Monde" ("Song of the World"), illustrating in a kind of modern Apocalypse the problems facing mankind in our day.
In the same building complex are a Romanesque cloister, a chapel and a small Wine Museum.

Location
Boulevard Arago

Opening times
1 July–14 Sept., daily
9 a.m.–noon and 2–6 p.m.;
15 Sept.–30 June, daily
10 a.m.–noon and 2–6 p.m.

Admission charge

Brissac

In the little town of Brissac (to the S of the Loire), set in a beautiful park, stands a château built in the early 17th c. on the site of an earlier building of the 13th–15th c. The château (open 9–11.30 a.m. and 2–6.30 p.m.; conducted tours) contains fine tapestries and 16th c. furniture.

Situation
16 km (10 miles) SE

Le Plessis-Bourré

The château of Le Plessis-Bourré, surrounded by a wide moat, has undergone little change since it was built in the 15th c. Laid out on a square plan, with round towers at the corners, it is entered by way of a bridge fully 40 m (130 ft) long. The château (Thurs.–Tues. 10 a.m.–noon and 2–5 p.m.; admission charge) has fine state apartments with period furniture; on the upper floor is an unusual painted wooden ceiling with allegorical representations.

Situation
20 km (12½ miles) N

Le Plessis-Macé

The château of Le Plessis-Macé, originally founded in the 11th c., dates in its present aspect mainly from the 15th c. It has a charming courtyard and a chapel in Flamboyant (Late Gothic) style.

Situation
15 km (9 miles) NW

Serrant

Serrant lies just off the main road (N23), to the S. The château, set in a beautiful park and surrounded by a moat, is a magnificent Renaissance building flanked by corner pavilions (16th–18th c.), in masonry which shows an attractive contrast between dark and light-coloured stone. Open Wed.–Mon. 9 a.m.–noon and 2–6 p.m. (conducted tours), it contains numerous works of art, tapestries and pictures, as well as a library.

Situation
18 km (11 miles) SW

Azay-le-Rideau

Region: Centre
Département: Indre-et-Loire
Altitude: 45 m (148 ft)
Population: 3000

Situation

The little town of Azay-le-Rideau lies some 25 km (15 miles) SW of Tours on the Indre, a left-bank tributary of the Loire, surrounded by attractive countryside.

History

The site was apparently already fortified in the very early medieval period. In 1518 Gilles Berthelot, a leading financier in the reign of François I, chose this beautiful spot for the erection of a château, built on the remains of the earlier castle which had been destroyed in 1418. He did not enjoy his elegant new residence for long, for he was compelled to flee in 1527 as the result of a financial scandal and his property fell to the crown.

** Château

Opening times
Palm Sunday–30 Sept., daily 9 a.m.–noon and 2–6.30 p.m.; 1 Oct.–15 Nov., daily 9 a.m.–noon and 2–5 p.m.; 16 Nov.–Palm Sunday, daily 9.30 a.m.–noon and 2–4.45 p.m.

Conducted tours

Admission charge

Son et lumière
See Practical Information

From the main road through the town a beautiful avenue runs S through the park, with its many old trees, to the château, built on an island in the Indre. It was originally intended to have four wings laid out on a square plan, but Berthelot had time only to complete the main building and the shorter W wing. In its present form, however, Azay-le-Rideau is one of the most beautiful and harmonious of the Loire châteaux.

Although what first strikes the visitor in this Early Renaissance building is the massive corner towers, the elegant façade with its rows of windows shows that the château was designed not for defensive purposes but for show and elegant social life. Even the moat had no defensive function. A wall-walk with machicolations (openings between corbels) runs round the top of the walls; but even this military feature is pure decoration, designed to enhance the commanding aspect of the building.

Exterior

On the entrance front the stairwell, in a style showing the influence of the Italian Renaissance, projects slightly from the façade which is topped by a gable: an innovation compared with the previous practice, which was to link the different floors of a building by spiral staircases contained in built-on towers. Above the two doors are the emblems of François I and his queen, the salamander and the ermine.

The S and W fronts are reflected in the water of the Indre, which here flows through the wide moat. Adjoining is the extensive park of the château. Dramatic presentations in period costume take place here on summer evenings.

Interior

An interesting feature of the ground floor is the kitchen with its rib-vaulted roof; the chimney and the well lie below the level of the floor, which was raised in a later period. The dining room, with a heavy beamed ceiling, contains Flemish tapestries; the massive and richly decorated chimneypiece was designed by Auguste Rodin (1840–1917), following old models. The furniture is copied from period pieces. There are more tapestries in other rooms on the ground floor.

On the first floor is the Chambre du Roi (King's Bedroom). In front of the fireplace can be seen the original stone floor; the parquet was laid on the occasion of a visit by Louis XIV. By the fireplace is a travelling secretaire decorated with ivory and gold leaf. The Reception Room, beyond the staircase, is the largest room in the château. On the chimneypiece is a salamander painted in trompe-l'œil technique and on the walls are four large tapestries depicting Biblical scenes. Adjoining, in the side wing to the right, is a room containing excellently preserved

Son et lumière   *Stairwell, Azay-le-Rideau*

18th c. tapestries; the windows have tinted glass to protect the tapestries from the sun.

The stairwell has a notable stone ceiling, partly rib-vaulted, partly coffered with portrait medallions or foliage ornament.

Church of St-Symphorien

The little church of St-Symphorien, mainly Romanesque in style but with Gothic vaulting, is situated to the S of the town centre (reached by way of Rue Balzac and Rue Gambetta). On the façade of the right-hand aisle are remains of a Carolingian relief. The left-hand part of the façade is Late Gothic, with some features marking the transition to the Renaissance.

Location
Place du 11-Novembre-1918

La Baule

Region: Pays de la Loire
Département: Loire-Atlantique
Altitude: sea level
Population: 15,000

Situation

The town of La Baule, founded as recently as 1879 but now ranking next to Biarritz as the leading resort on the French Atlantic coast, lies NW of the estuary of the Loire and thus, geographically, belongs to Brittany. It is surrounded by salt-pans and pinewoods planted to consolidate the dunes.

*Beach

The sandy beach, several kilometres long, is one of the finest in the whole of France. Since the Loire is navigable only near its mouth and has suffered relatively little pollution from industrial waste water, and since the tides maintain regular circulation and exchange, the quality of the water is good.
The principal hotels and the Casino lie on the broad seafront promenade. Just off the promenade, set amid shady trees, are many attractive villas.

Parc des Dryades

Location
E of town

To the E of the town centre of La-Baule-les-Pins, many of the houses of which are scattered about in the pinewoods, is the Parc des Dryades, a botanical garden containing many exotic species.

Guérande

Situation
6 km (4 miles) N

To the N of La Baule, reached by way of the "salt town" of Saillé amid the extensive salt-pans, is the little town of Guérande, still ringed by well-preserved medieval walls. In Place St-Aubin stands the church of St Aubin (12th–16th c.), with figured Romanesque capitals. A little way SE of the church the Porte St-Michel, one of the old town gates, now houses a small museum (regional history, folk traditions).

Guérande peninsula

Extent
10 km (6 miles) W

An attractive excursion from La Baule is to the Guérande peninsula, which projects into the Atlantic on the S side of a bay which is now silted up and covered with salt-pans.

Le Pouliguen

Immediately beyond the boating harbour is the modern resort of Le Pouliguen, on the section of coast known as the "Grande Côte" (many blocks of apartments).

Batz-sur-Mer

In the centre of the next little town, Batz-sur-Mer, stands the church of St-Guénolé, which was largely rebuilt in the 15th and 16th c. From its tower, and from the Sentier des Douaniers

(Path of the Customs Men), which starts from the Boulevard de la Mer, there are fine views of the coast.

The road then curves the rocky tip of the peninsula to the busy little fishing town and holiday resort of Le Croisic.
At the N end of the town, near the harbour, is the hill called Mont-Esprit, built up from the stones brought in as ballast by the salt ships. Although the hill is only 30 m (100 ft) high it affords a charming panoramic view.

Le Croisic

Beaugency

Region: Centre
Département: Loiret
Altitude: 110 m (361 ft)
Population: 7000

The old-world little town of Beaugency lies on the right bank of the Loire half-way between Orléans and Blois, in a predominantly agricultural region.
The main features of interest are all close together near the river in the old town, of which there is a good view from the bridge.

Situation

Château

The Château Dunois was built in the 15th c. by the Comte de Dunois, the "Bastard of Orléans". It now houses the Musée Régional, with collections of folk material (costumes, craftsmen's tools and agricultural implements), sections devoted to viticulture and toys, and mementoes of local celebrities, including the novelist Eugène Sue (1804–57), whose novels of low life and crime (e.g. "Les mystères de Paris") brought him an international reputation.

Location
Place Dunois

Opening times
1 Apr.–31 Oct.,
9–11.30 a.m. and 2–6 p.m.;
1 Oct.–31 Mar.,
9–11.30 a.m. and 2–4 p.m.

Conducted tours

Admission charge

Adjoining the château is a massive rectangular keep 36 m (118ft) high, a relic of an earlier castle (11th c.). Only the outer walls survive; the interior is not accessible.

Son et lumière
See Practical Information

Church of Notre-Dame

The church of Notre-Dame, originally an abbey church, was built in the 12th c., but lost its unity of style when it was partly rebuilt in Gothic style after a fire. It has an aisled interior, with a transept which consists merely of a heightening of the vaulting over the aisles and does not project from the side walls. Under the crossing is the altar, and behind it, in the apse, a Romanesque font. The massive round piers in the nave have sparse figural ornament.

Location
Place Dunois

Tour St-Firmin

In the triangular Place St-Firmin, a few paces W of the church, stands the 50 m (164 ft) high Tour St-Firmin, the only remnant of a 16th c. church which was destroyed during the French Revolution.

Location
Place St-Firmin

Old town

To the NW of the château extends the picturesque old town, with a number of fine old buildings. Among them are the Maison des Templiers (Templars' House) in Rue Prateau, the Hôtel de Ville (Town Hall) in Rue du Change and, farther along that street to the NW, the Tour de l'Horloge, a clock tower which was formerly incorporated in the town walls.

Avaray

Situation
13 km (8 miles) SW

As early as the 13th c. Avaray had a castle, which later frequently became a residence of the French kings. Rebuilt after 1736, it preserves only the four corner towers of the original structure. On the opposite bank of the Loire is an atomic power station.

Talcy

Situation
15 km (9 miles) W

The village of Talcy lies in the plain some distance from the Loire. The best approach is from Avaray to Mer and from there on D15.
Of the château of Talcy, built in the 15th–16th c., there remain only one wing and a tower. The interior has preserved its original form, with period furniture.

Blois

Region: Centre
Département: Loir-et-Cher
Altitude: 72 m (236 ft)
Population: 52,000

Situation

Blois, chief town of the département of Loir-et-Cher, lies on two hills on the steep right bank of the Loire, some 60 km (37 miles) SW of Orléans, in the centre of a rich farming area.

History

In the 11th and 12th c. the Counts of Blois and Champagne were among the most influential feudal lords in France. In 1397 the county passed to Louis d'Orléans, whose eldest son Charles, after returning from 25 years in English captivity, pulled down part of the old fortified castle and built in its place a new residential wing. When Louis XII, a scion of the house of Orléans, came to the throne this marked the beginning of a period of great splendour for the château, which was the king's favourite residence. He added additional wings and laid out extensive terraced gardens to the NW, in an area now occupied by houses. This building activity was continued in the reign of François I.

Doorway of the Château de Blois, with equestrian statue of Louis XII ▶

During the Wars of Religion, in 1588, the château was the scene of a bloody deed. The Duc de Guise, Henri III's rival and leader of the Catholic League, had compelled the king to call a meeting of the States General in Blois. Since almost all the members of the assembly had been brided by the duke, he was confident that he could achieve his main object and bring about the dethronement of the king; but Henri anticipated his move and had him murdered on 23 December 1588. The king himself, however, lived for only another eight months.

** Château

Location
Place du Château

Opening times
16 Mar.–30 Sept.,
daily 9 a.m.–noon and
2–6.30 p.m.
1 Oct.–15 Mar.,
daily 9 a.m.–noon and
2–5 p.m.

Conducted tours
If desired (in English as well as French)

Admission charge

Son et lumière
See Practical Information

François I Wing

The château, a massive square structure open only on the SE side, occupies a commanding situation above the town. From the lower town a street ascends to the Place du Château (car parking), the SW side of which is occupied by the entrance front of the Château (the Louis XII Wing, 1498–1503). Above the main and side doorways is Louis XII's emblem, the crowned porcupine; and in a canopied recess with a profusion of Late Gothic ornament over the main doorway is an equestrian statue of Louis XII, a 19th c. copy of the original.

Entering the large inner courtyard through the Louis XII Wing, we see on the right the François I Wing, with the celebrated spiral staircase. Diagonally opposite, at right angles to the François I Wing, is the Gaston d'Orléans Wing, in classical style, designed by François Mansart.
To the left of this wing is an opening which gives access to a small terrace. The rest of this side of the château is occupied by the low Galerie Charles d'Orléans and the Chapel.

The three-story François I Wing, built in the early 16th c., has a richly decorated façade showing the influence of contemporary Italian art, and thus representing a departure from the medieval French architectural tradition.
The architectural showpiece of this wing is the monumental spiral staircase, housed in an octagonal tower projecting from the façade. It was originally in the centre of the façade, which was later shortened by the construction of the Gaston d'Orléans Wing. When court ceremonies and festivals were held in the courtyard the open galleries of the staircase served as boxes for spectators.
The François I Wing contains a series of splendid state apartments, though the present decoration and furnishings date mostly from the 19th c. The floor tiles still show traces of their original coloured glaze. Among the rooms which are still more or less in their original state is the Salle d'Honneur on the first floor, with a large and richly decorated chimneypiece bearing the salamander of François I and the ermine of Anne de Bretagne, emblems which recur all over the château.
Adjoining are the apartments of Catherine de Médicis. The wooden panelling of her Cabinet (closet), at the far end of her suite of rooms, beyond the chapel, conceals secret compartments which could be opened only by means of a hidden pedal. On the second floor are the apartments of Henri III. The rooms facing the outside were the scene of the Duc de Guise's murder on 23 December 1588; it is said that Henri watched the deed from his study, hidden behind a curtain. The sequence of events is shown on a plan on the wall.

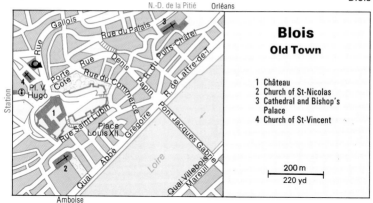

Blois
Old Town

1 Château
2 Church of St-Nicolas
3 Cathedral and Bishop's
  Palace
4 Church of St-Vincent

200 m
220 yd

Amboise

At the end of the wing, adjoining the entrance front, is the Salles des Etats-Géneraux (Hall of the States General). measuring 30×18 m (98×59 ft) and reaching up through two storeys. It is divided by a row of columns into two vaulted aisles. Here, too, the decoration and furnishings date from the 19th c. On the walls are huge 17th and 18th c. tapestries, two of them depicting the exploits of Louis XIV, the other three episodes from the life of Constantine the Great (c. 280–337). From here we can reach the Museum in the Louis XII Wing.

The two-storey Louis XII Wing occupies the entrance front of the château, continuing round the SE side of the courtyard, adjoining the Chapel. On the ground floor of this wing, built about 1500 of red brick and light-coloured stone, is an arcaded gallery, and at the S angle is a staircase tower. The wing now houses the Musée des Beaux-Arts (Museum of Fine Art; open daily 9 a.m.–12.30 p.m. and 2–5.30 p.m.), with pictures (mainly by Italian, French and Flemish artists), sculpture, porcelain and 16th–19th c. costume.

Louis XII Wing

The Chapel is built on to the SE part of the Louis XII Wing. Aisleless, with ribbed vaulting, it is decorated with painted coats of arms. The windows are modern. To the right is a polychrome Gothic Virgin. The Bourbon fleur-de-lis and a stylised ermine's tail constantly recur in the floor pavement, particularly in the chancel, and are found also in the coat of arms above the door lintel.
Beside the chapel doorway is a small terrace from which there is a fine view of the lower town, with the church of St-Nicolas (see below) in the foreground.

Chapel

This three-storey wing, on the SW side of the courtyard, was built in 1635–38 by François Mansart, the leading architect of the French classical school. Its construction involved the demolition of part of the François I Wing and the chapel, which was originally much larger. The wing remained unfurnished, and the original plan to rebuild and enlarge the whole château in the same style was never carried out.
The Gaston d'Orléans Wing is not open to the public.

Gaston d'Orléans Wing

The world-famed Grand Staircase   *Church of St-Nicolas*

Church of St-Nicolas

Location
Rue des Trois-Marchands

To the S of the Château is the church of St-Nicolas, built in the 12th and 13th c. and originally belonging to a Benedictine abbey. The conventual buildings, rebuilt between 1663 and 1724 and now secularised, lie to the SE. The columns in the choir and transept have interesting Romanesque figured capitals. The nave is predominantly Gothic.

Cathédrale St-Louis

Location
Place St-Louis

The Cathedral stands in the old town to the NE of the Château. It occupies the site of a church built in early Christian times and rebuilt or restored in the 12th, 15th and 16th c. In 1678 the whole church apart from the apse, the tower and the W front was destroyed in a hurricane; the rebuilding, ordered by Colbert, took until 1702. The present Cathedral is Late Gothic and Renaissance, with the exception of the base of the tower, a relic of the 12th c. church.

The interior is 80 m (262 ft) long, 30 m (98 ft) wide and up to 18.70 m (61 ft) high. The beautiful crypt dates from the 10th–11th c.

Bishop's Palace

Adjoining the apse of the Cathedral is the old Bishop's Palace (18th c.), now the Town Hall. From the gardens to the E there is a charming view.

Old Town

The old part of the town, to the S of the Cathedral, is attractive and picturesque, with some interesting old burghers' houses.

Church of Notre-Dame de la Trinité

The church of Notre-Dame de la Trinité, consecrated in 1949, lies outside the town centre to the NE. Notable features of the interior are the Stations of the Cross and the stained-glass windows.
The tower, 60 m (197 ft) high, contains a carillon. From the top (reached by a staircase) there is a fine panoramic view.

Location
Rue Monin

Château-Renault

In the little town of Château-Renault are the ruins of 14th c. castle, with an even older keep. Within the castle precincts is a small Leather Museum.

Situation
34 km (21 miles) W

Ménars

The village of Ménars lies on the right bank of the Loire. It has a château, set in beautiful terraced gardens, which was originally built in the mid 17th c. for a prosperous citizen named Guillaume Charron. In 1716 it was acquired by the Marquise de Pompadour, who had it enlarged by the court architect Gabriel. In the mid 18th c. extensive alterations were carried out. It now ranks among the very few examples of the French classical style in the Loire valley.

Situation
6 km (4 miles) NE

Bourges

Region: Centre
Département: Cher
Altitude: 130 m (427 ft)
Population: 80,000

Bourges, chief town of the département of Cher, the see of an archbishop and a former ducal capital, lies in the fertile region of Berry, some 50 km (30 miles) from the Loire, to the W of Nevers and La Charité. The Yèvre, a tributary of the Cher, flows through the town.

Situation

In Gallo-Roman times the town, which was taken by Caesar in 52 B.C., was known as Avaricum. In the early Middle Ages it was the chief town of a country, and about 1360 it became the residence and capital of the Dukes of Berry and developed into a widely renowned centre of art and culture. The University was founded in 1463, and about 1530 the reformer Jean Calvin was a student there. While at the University he heard from German fellow-students about the ideas put forward by Luther, which made a deep impression on him and made Bourges the starting-point of the Reformation in Berry.
During the Wars of Religion, in 1562, the town was taken by the Protestants. In 1753–54 the Parlement de Paris was exiled to Bourges. Industrialisation came to Bourges in the mid 19th c. and chemical works and the aircraft industry now make major contributions to its economy.

History

Bourges

**Cathédrale St-Etienne

Location
Place Etienne-Dolet

Opening times
Mon.–Sat. 10–11.30 a.m.
and 2–6 p.m.,
Sun. 2–6 p.m. (crypt and
tower)

Admission charge
(Crypt and tower)

Façade

Bourges' magnificent Cathedral, one of the finest in France, is conspicuously situated on the hill rising out of the plain which is occupied by the oldest part of the town. It was built between 1200 and 1260.

The W front, flanked by two massive towers, is 55 m (180 ft) wide and has five doorways with rich figural decoration. The doorway farthest to the left (N) is the Portail St-Guillaume (St William's), named after a former archbishop of Bourges. In the tympanum are scenes from the saint's life (miraculous healings, expulsion of devils, etc.). The next doorway is the Portail de la Vierge, dedicated to the

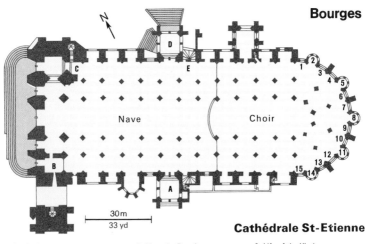

Bourges

Cathédrale St-Etienne

A South doorway		St Mary the Egyptian	8 Life of the Virgin
B Sacristy		3 Legend of St Stephen	9 Last Judgement
C Ticket office		4 The Good Samaritan	10 The Passion
Entrance to tower		5 SS. Denis (Dionysius),	11 SS. Lawrence, Stephen
D N doorway		Peter, Paul and Martin	and Vincent
E Entrance to crypt		6 Parable of the Prodigal	12 Revelation of St John
		Son	13 The Apostle Thomas
STAINED GLASS		7 The Old and the New	14 SS. James the Greater,
1 Dives and Lazarus		Covenant: Abraham,	John the Baptist and
2 Mary Magdalene, St		Isaac, Moses, David and	John the Evangelist
Nicholas and		Jonah	15 Joseph in Egypt

Virgin. It was badly damaged when the N tower collapsed in 1506 and was rebuilt in the style of the 16th c. The tympanum depicts the death, assumption and coronation of the Virgin.

The commanding central doorway has a finely conceived last Judgement. Above it is a 14th c. rose window.

The doorway next to the right is the Portail St-Etienne (St Stephen's), with scenes from the life and martyrdom of St Stephen (to whom the Cathedral is dedicated).

The fifth doorway is the Portail St-Ursin (St Ursinus's). The sculpture in the tympanum depicts the legend of St Ursinus, first bishop of Bourges.

The figures on the piers between the doorways are modern.

The N tower, 65 m (213 ft) high, was rebuilt in Flamboyant (Late Gothic) style after its collapse in 1506. It is well worth making the ascent of the tower (entrance and ticket offices inside the Cathedral: see plan, p. 50).

Towers

Cathedral and Bishop's Palace, Bourges

The S tower, set slightly to one side of the Cathedral and linked with it by an intermediate structure, is in a severer style. It was left unfinished and falls short of the height originally planned.

The Cathedral is entered by the Romanesque doorway (12th c.) on the S side. Above the doorway, on the outer wall, is a Maiestas Domini (Christ enthroned), surrounded by the symbols of the four Evangelists. On the central pier is a figure of Christ in the attitude of blessing (13th c.).

Interior

The interior, 124 m (407 ft) long, consists of the nave, 37 m (121 ft) high, and two aisles of different heights on each side.

The aisles are continued by a double ambulatory with radial chapels round the choir; there is no transept.

* * Stained glass

The most striking feature of the Cathedral is the brilliant 13th c. stained glass in the choir chapels. In view of the wealth of detail in the windows the use of binoculars is recommended, particularly for the higher windows.
There is also some fine stained glass (15th and 16th c.) in the side chapels.

* * Crypt

The entrance to the crypt (conducted visit; tickets for crypt and tower at W end of N aisle) is by the N doorway, which is normally closed. The Gothic crypt (12th c.) was constructed under the choir in order to allow for the difference in level at the edge of the town, on the Gallo-Roman walls. As a result the crypt is above ground level and provided with an abundance of light by twelve large windows.
In the crypt is the fine marble tomb of the Duc de Berry (with a bear at his feet), which dates from the early 14th c. – all that remains of a large mausoleum. Here, too, are a few fragments of the old rood-loft.
Inscribed on the floor can be seen a full-scale working drawing for the rose window on the W front, which was put together in the crypt. Note the asymmetric form of the ribbed vaulting, adapted to the semicircular ground plan.
In the Gothic crypt are the tombs of bishops and archbishops of Bourges (with two places still unoccupied). Beside a polychrome Entombment (16th c.) is the entrance to the small Romanesque crypt, which lies within the Gallo-Roman walls and has become accessible only in recent years.

Bishop's Palace

Location
Place Etienne-Dolet

Facing the Cathedral, to the S, stands the former Bishop's Palace (1680), now the Hôtel de Ville (Town Hall). The beautiful gardens adjoining (Jardin de l'Archevêché) were laid out in the 17th c., it is believed by the famous landscape gardener Le Nôtre. From here there is a very instructive view of the S side and the apse of the Cathedral.
At the S end of the gardens, in Place du 8-Mai, is the Maison de la Culture (House of Culture), with a "stabile" by Alexander Calder in front of it.

Hôtel Lallemant

Location
Rue Bourbonnoux

Opening times
1 Apr.–15 Oct.,
Tues.–Sun. 10–11.15 a.m.
and 2–5.15 p.m.;
16 Oct.–31 Mar.,
Tues.–Sun. 10–11.15 a.m.
and 2–4.15 p.m.

Conducted tours

Admission charge

Going E through the Jardin de l'Archevêché, we come into Rue Bourbonnoux, an attractive street in the old town. Some 250 m (275 yd) N along this street is the Hôtel Lallemant, a handsome 16th c. merchant's house. It was built on the remains of the Gallo-Roman walls, and accordingly parts of the house are on different levels. The street front with its Gothic windows already shows the influence of the Renaissance in its central section, and this style is fully developed in the design of the inner courtyards. The house now contains a museum, with furniture, tapestries and pictures (mainly 17th c.).
There are fine coffered ceilings in the residential apartments and the chapel. The porcupines and ermines on the chimneypieces are the emblems of Louis XII and Anne de Bretagne.

Stained glass

Palais Jacques-Cœur

Church of St-Bonnet

The church of St-Bonnet, a little way NE of the Hôtel Lallemant, has a 16th c. choir and beautiful windows of the 15th and 16th c.

Location
Place St-Bonnet

Palais Jacques-Cœur

The imposing Palais Jacques-Cœur, to the W of the Hôtel Lallemant through the streets of the old town, was built in 1443–53 for the financier and royal treasurer Jacques Cœur, whose punning emblems – St James's cockleshell (*coquille St-Jacques*) and a heart (*cœur*) – are constantly repeated decorative features all over the building.
While the W front still has the forbidding aspect of a fortified house, the street front shows the showy elegance of the late Gothic and early Renaissance periods. Note, above the doorway, the blind windows with human figures and, below the windows, the small portrait heads. In the small square in front of the palace is a 19th c. monument to Jacques Cœur.
The palace is laid out in an irregular square around a magnificent courtyard with three richly ornamented staircase towers giving access to the upper floors.

The conducted tour begins on the ground floor of the rear wing (residential apartments: the wing facing the street contains the former business premises). The Grande Salle has an unusual

Location
Rue Jacques-Cœur

Opening times
Whitsun–31 Oct.,
daily 9.15–11.10 a.m. and
2.15–5.10 p.m.;
2 Nov.–Whitsun,
daily 10.15–11.10 a.m. and
2.15–4.10 p.m.

Conducted tours

Admission charge

Interior

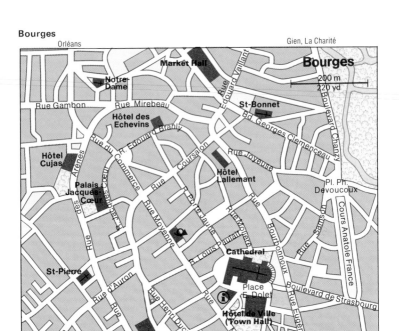

chimneypiece decorated with monkeys, hares, wild pigs and other animals. Opposite it is a loggia for musicians, with painted decoration.

Passing through the Turkish Bath, we go up to the first floor. In an antechamber on this floor is the only surviving stained-glass window in the house, representing a galley. The same theme is repeated above the door.

Parallel to the suite of rooms beyond this is a narrow corridor which enabled the master of the house to reach any of the rooms without being seen.

From the Salle du Conseil (used as a courtroom in the 19th c. when the palace housed the town hall and law courts) we pass into the Galerie des Marchands, with a timber ceiling in the form of an upturned boat.

The Chapel has magnificent ceiling frescoes of 1488, long hidden by a false ceiling. In the Salle d'Audience are two chimneypieces with figural decoration, one depicting a castle and a tournament, with spectators looking on, and the other a peasants' tournament with donkeys as mounts, sticks instead of lances and basketwork shields. There is also a group showing Jacques Cœur and his wife playing chess.

Hôtel Cujas

This handsome Renaissance mansion, built about 1515, stands on the W side of the old town, near the Palais Jacques-Cœur. It now houses the Musée du Berry, a regional museum with a large collection of material on the history of Berry, including prehistoric and Gallo-Roman times. Two other items of interest are the material illustrating life in town and country in the 18th and 19th c. and a large collection of work by Jean Boucher (1568–1633), who was active as a painter in Bourges.

Location
Rue des Arènes

Opening times
Daily 9 a.m.–noon and 2–6 p.m.

Admission charge

Church of Notre-Dame

The church of Notre Dame, on the N side of the old town, was originally built in the 15th c., and was rebuilt in 1520–23 following its destruction in a great fire 1487. Its architecture shows different phases in the transition from Gothic to Renaissance.

Location
Rue Notre-Dame

To the S of the church is the Hôtel Pellevoysin (15th–16th c.), in which the architect of the Cathedral is said to have lived.

Hôtel Pellevoysin

Hôtel des Echevins

SE of the church of Notre-Dame, in the old town, is the Hôtel des Echevins, built in the late 15th c. as a meeting-place for the mayor and municipal magistrates. Notable features are the octagonal staircase tower in Flamboyant (Late Gothic) style and the Renaissance gallery, built some 20 years later.

Location
Rue Branly

Chambord

Region: Centre
Département: Loir-et-Cher
Altitude: 70 m (230 ft)

The imposing Château de Chambord, the largest of the Loire châteaux, lies some 15 km (9 miles) E of Blois on the Cosson, a left-bank tributary of the Loire. The château is set in a huge park with dense stands of old trees.

Situation

The forests of Sologne, as this area in the bend of the Loire is known, were celebrated hunting grounds before the château was built. François I resolved to erect a château here which should be exactly as he wished it, and building began in 1519. Work stopped, however, when François was taken prisoner by the Emperor Charles V in the battle of Pavia. It was resumed after the king was released on giving up his territorial claims in Italy, and thereafter proceeded apace, continuing well into the reign of Henri II.
Here in 1552 was signed the treaty of Chambord, under which Henri undertook to support Duke Moritz of Saxony (1521–33: not to be confused with the later Moritz of Saxony, known as

History

the Maréchal de Saxe) in his planned rising against the Emperor. In return Henri was granted control of the three bishoprics of Metz, Toul and Verdun – the prelude to the incorporation of these territories in France.

Louis XIV frequently resided in Chambord and attracted leading writers and artists of the day to his court, including the great dramatist Molière (1622–73) and the composer Jean-Baptiste Lully or Lulli (1623–87), a native of Florence, who wrote music for many of Molière's plays.

In 1748 Louis XV presented this valuable property to Count Moritz of Saxony, known as the Maréchal de Saxe (1696–1750), as a reward for his victory over the Austrians in the battle of Fontenoy; but only two years later, on the Marshal's death, Chambord reverted to the crown. During the French Revolution no significant damage was caused to the château, but almost all its contents were sold. Since 1932 Chambord has been the property of the state.

*Château

Opening times
1 Apr.–19 June,
daily 9.30 a.m.–noon and
2–6 p.m.;
20 June–31 Aug.,
daily 9.30 a.m.–noon and
2–7 p.m.;

The château forms a large rectangle measuring 156 m (512 ft) wide and 117 m (384 ft) long. Although the layout, with a central keep and massive round towers at the corners, still shows some of the characteristics of a defensive structure, the desire to achieve an effect of magnificence is clearly predominant. In size and architectural conception Chambord

Château de Chambord, NW front

anticipates the absolutist claim to authority which was later to attain full expression in palaces such as Versailles. It was even part of the original plan to divert the Loire, 5 km (3 miles) away, to make it serve as a (purely decorative) moat; but in the event the more modest plan of canalising the Cosson, in which the château is now mirrored, was adopted instead. (For Son et lumière, see Practical Information.)

Visitors approaching the château by the route recommended in this Guide will, after a delightful drive through the park (see p. 50), catch sight in the first place of the NW front, with its two flanking round towers and the twin towers of the keep rising in the middle. From this point the most striking characteristic of the château is already evident – the extraordinary profusion of turrets, chimneys and lanterns which over the years have been added to the roof.

From the car park (near which are souvenir shops, a restaurant, etc.), passing a chapel built in the time of Napoleon I, we come to the SE front of the château, with the Porte Royale. This wing was never completed; it consists merely of the flat-roofed ground floor and the bases of the two corner towers. It is occupied in part by stables and a smithy; to the right is a small theatre.

The Porte Royale leads into the Cour d'Honneur (Grand Courtyard), which in spite of the limited height of the SE front seems cramped and constricted. In the centre is the massive Donjon (Keep), the NW side of which is incorporated in the outer wall of the château. The Keep has no defensive function,

1 Sept.–31 Oct.,
daily 9.30 a.m.–noon and
2–6 p.m.;
1 Nov.–31 Mar.,
daily 9.30 a.m.–noon and
2–5 p.m.

Admission charge

Exterior

Chambord

Ornamental chimneys

Spiral staircase

its walls being opened up and articulated by numerous windows, galleries and balustrades. On the high-pitched gabled roof are no fewer than 365 ornamental chimneys, lanterns and turrets.

The interior of the château makes it evident that the whole building was designed for show, with no concessions to comfort or convenience. Altogether there are some 400 rooms. The numerous pictures are mostly copies of museum pieces. On the ground floor of the Keep only the Salle des Gardes (Guard Room) is furnished and open to the public. This consists of four halls disposed in the form of a cross, with the celebrated spiral staircase in the centre. The staircase is really two staircases in one, fitted into one another in such a way that a person going up one staircase would not meet anyone coming down on the other: an arrangement which was probably conceived as a Baroque refinement rather than a diplomatic necessity.

On the walls of the staircase, on the first floor, are hangings painted with the family trees of the houses of Valois and Bourbon-Parma, together with a bird's-eye view of the château and surrounding area.

A series of rooms on the first floor are open to visitors. A small dark panelled anteroom leads into the Chambre du Roi (King's Bedroom), decorated in Baroque style by the Maréchal de Saxe, a portrait bust of whom is on the chimneypiece. The adjoining room contains a collection of portraits and a console table on the inner end wall which is the only item surviving from the original furnishings of the château. The other rooms contain tapestries and pictures. The Chambre au Laurier Rose has woven wall hangings patterned with rose laurel on a white ground. A large case in the Chambre du Dauphin contains models of cannon, siege engines, etc.

In contrast to the lower floors the second floor has coffered stone vaulting rather than a timber ceiling. Everywhere on the ceiling is to be seen François I's salamander and initial F. The various rooms contain a large collection of weapons and hunting trophies, together with works by 17th c. Flemish animal painters and tapestries depicting the legend of Meleager.

The staircase continues up to the roof, with a terrace fitted in between tall gables. The staircase itself is topped by a lantern. A walk round the roof reveals the bewildering abundance and variety of the decorative features which were added by each successive architect; the visitor feels lost in some fantastic little town. Some of Molière's plays are said to have been given their first performance here. A balustrade runs round the edge of the roof, from which there are fine views in all directions of the château and its park.

In addition to the rooms in the Keep a classical-style chapel on the first floor of the left-hand side wing (reached by a spiral staircase at the angle of the building) is open to visitors.

Chapel

Round the château extends the Parc de Chambord, an area of 5407 hectares (13,355 acres), mostly wooded, which is enclosed by a 32 km (20 mile) long wall with six gates. It is now a reserve for deer and wild boar, and only a small part of it, therefore, is open to the public. At some points the animals can be seen being fed in the morning and evening.

*Park

La Charité-sur-Loire

Region: Bourgogne
Département: Nièvre
Altitude: 175 m (574 ft)
Population: 6000

The little town of La Charité lies on the right bank of the Loire some 25 km (15 miles N) of Nevers. Its river harbour was of some economic importance until the 19th c.

Situation

*Church of Notre-Dame

The church of Notre-Dame originally belonged to a Benedictine abbey, the buildings of which, dating from the 11th–12th c., have now almost completely disappeared. Although only part of the church survives, it ranks among the finest examples of Romanesque architecture in Burgundy.

Location
Place des Pêcheurs

Of the W front, facing on the Place des Pêcheurs, there remain the badly damaged central doorway, the side doorway (now walled up) on the right and the sturdy Romanesque tower to the left. In the left-hand tympanum is a frieze depicting the

Exterior

Romanesque arcades, La Charité

Annunciation, the Visitation, the Nativity and the shepherds in the fields; above is a badly damaged figure of Christ in a mandorla (a pointed oval aureole). Beyond the doorway, in the base of the tower (to left), is a model of the church as it once was.

In front of the classical-style entrance to the church a series of Romanesque arcades from the old nave can be seen on the top floor of two houses on the left.

The present church incorporates the E end of the original one. The nave was largely rebuilt in the 17th c., but the choir and transept are still much as they were. Above the crossing is an octagonal tower.

Interior

The finely proportioned interior of the church, which is built of light-coloured limestone, is free of later additions and is of impressive spatial effect. Except over the N aisle it has a vaulted roof.

In the S aisle the foundations of an earlier church have been exposed. The S transept has an excellently preserved tympanum with a carved frieze which is the counterpart of the one already mentioned, depicting (below) the Three Kings and Jesus in the Temple and (above) the Transfiguration. The columns in the ambulatory round the choir have fine figured capitals.

Square des Bénédictins

From this little square to the E of the church there is a good view of the nave. The remains of an earlier church (11th c.) are exposed here.

Museum

To the NW of the church, beside the Parc Adam, a small museum (open Wed.–Mon. 3–6 p.m., July and August also 10 a.m.–noon), houses material recovered by excavation in the town and collections devoted to local history and folk traditions.

Location
Rue des Chapelains

Admission charge

Châteaudun

Region: Centre
Département: Eure-et-Loir
Altitude: 140 m (459 ft)
Population: 16,000

The little town of Châteaudun lies some 50 km (30 miles) NW of Orléans, situated on higher ground above the Loir, a tributary of the Sarthe. The regular geometrical layout of the town centre is the result of its planned rebuilding after a fire in 1723.

Situation

The site was originally occupied by a Celtic settlement which was later taken by the Romans. From the 10th c. it belonged to the Counts of Blois, and in the 15th it passed to the "Bastard of Orléans", the Comte de Dunois, famous as a companion in arms of Jeanne d'Arc and a commander in the Hundred Years War. Dunois had the old fortified castle extensively rebuilt.
During the Franco-German War of 1870–71 the town was bombarded, set on fire and captured by Prussian troops.

History

*Chatêau

The magnificent château which gives the town its name stands on a crag falling steeply down to the Loir, to the NW of the old town. It consists of two wings set at right angles to one another, their outer walls rising to 60 m (200 ft) above the valley. In the substructures of the W wing, below the level of the courtyard, are extensive cellars and other offices.
Opening times: Daily 9–11.30 a.m. and 2–6 p.m.

Location
Place Jehan-de-Dunois

Conducted tours

Admission charge

The Cour d'Honneur (Grand Courtyard) is entered from the SE. On the wall beside the ticket-office is painted the Dunois family tree.
The courtyard is enclosed by the massive keep (left), adjoining which is the Chapel, and the two main wings, the Aile Dunois and the Aile Longueville. To the right is a narrow passage giving access to the terrace, from which there is a charming view of the Loir.

Exterior

The Sainte-Chapelle, between the W wing and the keep, was built in 1464. It is on two floors, the lower floor being entered from the courtyard. Round the interior are Gothic figures of saints; in the right-hand side chapel is a fresco of the Last Judgement (15th c.).

Chapel

Châteaudun

W wing

The Aile Dunois, the three-storey W wing, was built by the Bastard of Orléans from 1460 onwards. In Flamboyant (late Gothic) style, it has two basement floors containing various offices (access by staircase; not included in conducted tour). The interior, with beams of pest-resistant chestnut wood, contains many Aubusson and Flemish tapestries. In 1793 the revolutionary tribunal was installed in one of the rooms, leaving its mark in the wooden barriers and the emblem of the Revolution.

Immediately under the roof is wall-walk with machicolations (openings between corbels), commanding a view of the valley far below.

N wing

The Aile Longueville on the N side of the courtyard, built by François de Longueville between 1511 and 1532, already shows the influence of the Italian Renaissance. The height of the staircase at the right-hand end suggests that additional storeys were originally planned; and the irregular edge of the masonry at the right-hand end also points to an intention to carry out further building. The interior of the N wing, which is linked with the W wing by the stairwell at the corner of the courtyard, is more handsomely proportioned. It contains fine tapestries, richly ornamented chimneypieces and other features of interest. The Renaissance staircase, fronted by loggias with coffered ceilings, has a profusion of decoration; the stone steps contain numerous fossils.

Old town

Location
S of château

In the old town – e.g. in Rue St-Lubin and Rue des Huileries – there remain a few houses which survived fires in 1723 and 1870.

Madeleine church

The Madeleine church is on the S side of the old town, built up against the town walls. Parts of the church, including the crypt and the S doorway with its figural sculpture, date from the Romanesque period.

New town

Location
E of château

The new town was laid out after a fire in 1723. The regular plan with streets intersecting at right angles, characteristic of many Baroque towns, was the work of Jules Hardouin, nephew of Louis XIV's famous architect Hardouin-Mansart.

Promenade du Mail

The tree-shaded Promenade du Mail along the N side of the new town follows the edge of the escarpment above the Loir, affording extensive views. On its S side is the Office du Tourisme (entrance in Rue Toufaire), housed in a building which also contains a small museum (prehistoric and medieval finds, collection of birds).

Chapelle Notre-Dame du Champdé

SE of the town centre, at the end of Rue Gambetta, is the cemetery, at the entrance to which is the façade of the chapel of Notre-Dame du Champdé, destroyed in the late 19th c. The doorway shows the rich ornamentation of the Flamboyant style.

Keep and chapel, Châteaudun

Courtyard, Chaumont

Chaumont-sur-Loire

Region: Centre
Département: Loir-et-Cher
Altitude: 65 m (213 ft)
Population: 1000

The village of Chaumont lies on the left bank of the Loire roughly half-way between Blois and Amboise. On higher ground above the houses straggling along the river stands the château with its massive round towers. It was built in the 15th and 16th c. on earlier foundations.

Situation

*Château

From the iron gates at the road junction in the main street of the village a pleasantly shady path leads up to the château, on the S side of which extends a park with tall centuries-old cedars. Round the outside walls runs a frieze with a constantly repeated sylised representation of a burning hill ("chaud mont", a punning allusion to the name of the château). Below the wall-walk on the towers can be seen the initials of Diane de Poitiers, who lived here after being forced by Catherine de Médicis to give up Chenonceau (see Chenonceaux).
A drawbridge leads to the entrance gateway, flanked by two round towers. Above, left, is a cardinal's hat, the attribute of Georges d'Amboise; to the right are the arms, supported by two

Opening times
1 Apr.–30 Sept.,
daily 9–11.20 a.m. and
1.30–5.20 p.m.;
1 Oct.–31 Mar.,
daily 10–11.20 a.m. and
1.30–3.20 p.m.

Conducted tours

Admission charge

Chaumont

Chaumont: entrance to the château

wild men, of Charles II d'Amboise, whose initials appear in the carved frieze. The gateway leads into the courtyard, which is open on the side overlooking the Loire (view of river). The well is decorated with reliefs of archers, coats of arms and helmets.

Interior

The conducted tour begins in the W wing, to the left of the entrance. Here the family arms and the burning hill recur constantly in the decoration. Items of particular interest include a collection of terracotta portrait medallions, several tapestries and Renaissance furniture.

On the first floor, above the gateway, is a small armoury. Adjoining, in the right-hand wing, is a room with a beautiful floor of coloured tiles and several tapestries. From here we pass through another room into the gallery of the Late Gothic chapel.

Stables

SW of the château we come to a square stable block built in 1877, with stalls for the horses, a harness room (displaying harness for draught horses) and a coach-house with four coaches.

The conical structure at one corner is much older; originally a pottery kiln, it was used from the late 19th c. as a riding school.

The "chaud mont"

Chenonceaux

Region: Centre
Département: Indre-et-Loire
Altitude: 65 m (213 ft)
Population: 500

The little village of Chenonceaux (the spelling Chenonceau is used only for the château) lies some 30 km (20 miles) E of Tours on the N bank of the Cher, a left-bank tributary of the Loire.

The château of Chenonceau was erected from 1513 onwards, on the site of an earlier building, by Thomas Bohier, a financial official in the reign of Charles VIII. When Bohier died he was considerably in debt to the royal treasury, and his heirs were compelled to cede the château to the crown. In 1547 Henri II presented it to his mistress Diane de Poitiers, and after his death it passed into the possession of Catherine de Médicis, who compelled her rival Diane to exchange it for Chaumont. Catherine originally planned a huge extension to the château, but in the event only the wing over the river was built. Thereafter Chenonceau was the scene of brilliant court entertainments, in which the surrounding gardens and park also played a part.

*Château

In spite of its small size Chenonceau ranks as one of the most beautiful of the Loire châteaux. The only feature reminiscent of the military architecture of earlier days is the separate Donjon (Keep); the rest of the château is of astonishing lightness and grace.
From the car park an avenue of plane-trees runs straight through dense woodland to the château, which is seen on entring the outer courtyard, guarded by two sphinxes. To the

Opening times
16 Mar.–15 Sept., daily
9 a.m.–7 p.m.;
16–30 Sept., daily
9 a.m.–6.30 p.m.;
1 Oct.–15 Mar., daily
9 a.m.–6 p.m.

Admission charge

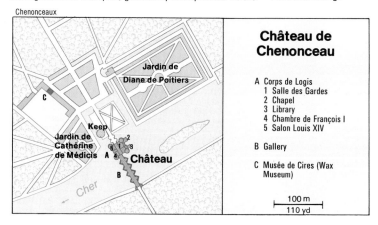

Chenonceaux

Château de Chenonceau

A Corps de Logis
  1 Salle des Gardes
  2 Chapel
  3 Library
  4 Chambre de François I
  5 Salon Louis XIV

B Gallery

C Musée de Cires (Wax Museum)

100 m
110 yd

Jardin de Diane de Poitiers

C

Keep

Jardin de Catherine de Médicis

A

Château

B

Cher

Chenonceau, Corps de Logis and Gallery

Son et lumière
See Practical Information

right are the gardens of Catherine de Médicis, to the left those of Diane de Poitiers. A bridge leads on to a square terrace surrounded by a moat, at the S corner of which is the Donjon (Keep). Beyond this a second bridge leads to the entrance to the château.

Exterior

The older part of the château, the Corps de Logis, built over the river, is flanked by four corner towers. It contains the former residential apartments, with the chapel at the NE corner. Beyond this, reaching almost to the other bank of the river, is the two-storey gallery wing (60m – 200 ft long), borne on four vaulted arches. In contrast to the Gothic-style vertical lines of the Corps de Logis, the emphasis here is on the horizontal. The window lintels and dormer windows (*lucarnes*) betray Italian influence.

Interior

Visitors first enter the entrance hall of the Corps de Logis, the axial corridor of which has Gothic vaulting. To the left is the Salle des Gardes (Guard Room), with a number of tapestries; it has a painted timber ceiling, the under sides of the beams being coffered. Off this room opens the Late Gothic chapel, with inscriptions (protected by glass) left by the Scots Guard. Above the door is the royal gallery. In a niche to the right is a Virgin and Child of Carrara marble.
From the Salle des Gardes we pass into the Chambre de Diane de Poitiers (Diane de Poitiers' Bedroom), with two large Flemish tapestries (16th c.). To the right, over the fireplace, hangs a portrait of Catherine de Médicis; to the left, by the window, a Virgin attributed to Murillo. Then (left) into the

Cabinet Vert (Green Closet), Catherine de Médicis' work-room or study, with the original painted wooden ceiling. It contains a number of notable pictures, including a "Queen of Sheba" of the school of Veronese. In the adjoining side-chamber, projecting over the river, is a small collection of medals.

The corridor leads into the Grand Gallery, which was used as a military hospital during the First World War (commemorative tablet on right-hand wall). On the walls are numerous portrait medallions. In the centre of the wooden ceiling, painted in monochrome, is a coffered section painted in black and grey – the colours of mourning in which part of the château was decorated by Louise of Lorraine after the murder of her husband Henri III in 1589.

To the right of the corridor is the Salon Louis XIV, with the salamander and ermine emblems on the chimneypiece. To the left is a portrait of the "Sun King" by Hyacinthe Rigaud (1659–1743). A small anteroom leads into the Chambre de François I (François I's Bedroom), with a magnificent Italian cabinet decorated in intarsia (mosaic woodwork). To the left of the window is a portrait of Diane de Poitiers as a huntress (Diana being the Roman goddess of hunting).

From the corridor a staircase leads down to the kitchen and other offices, in the piers supporting the gallery.

On the first floor the only rooms open to the public are those in the older part of the château; the upper floor of the gallery wing is not open. The vestibule contains a number of tapestries, and from the balcony there is a view of the avenue of plane-trees and the gardens. The rooms opening off the vestibule also have tapestries. The Chambre d'Estampes (Print Room) contains a collection of 18th and 19th c. engravings. The Chambre de César de Vendôme, with carved caryatids in the window embrasure, was restored in the 19th c.

The old stables now house a Wax Museum (Musée de Cires; open daily 9.45 a.m.–7 p.m.; admission charge), depicting events in the history of the château and surrounding area in 15 scenes with life-size wax figures.

Wax Museum

The gardens to left and right of the château were laid out anew in the 19th c. They afford excellent views of the château. Round the gardens extends a wooded park.

Gardens

Montrichard

The little town of Montrichard (the *t* is pronounced: Mon-Trichard), upstream from Chenonceaux on the right bank of the Cher, is dominated by an 11th c. fortified tower. In the old town centre are a number of well-preserved 16th c. houses and one, the Maison du Prêche, dating from the 11th c. On the W side of the town stands the fine pilgrimage church of Nanteuil (12th–13th and 15th c.; pilgrimage on Whit Monday).

Situation
8 km (5 miles) E

Cheverny

See Cour-Cheverny

Chinon

Region: Centre
Département: Indre-et-Cher
Altitude: 35 m (115 ft)
Population: 8000

Situation

Chinon lies 50 km (30 miles) SW of Tours on the right bank of the Vienne, a left-bank tributary of the Loire.

History

The spur of hill above the town, now occupied by the ruins of the château, was the site of a Gallo-Roman oppidum. This excellent strategic situation was also recognised in later centuries, and its defences were developed by the Counts of Blois in the 10th–11th c. and the Counts of Anjou in the 12th c. Through Henry of Anjou (later Henry II), the first Plantagenet, Chinon passed into English hands (1154). In 1205 the French king Philippe Auguste besieged and captured the castle, and thereafter strengthened it still further.

The most important event in Chinon's history was the meeting of Jeanne d'Arc and King Charles VII on 9 March 1429, which marked the beginning of the reconquest of French territory from the English. After Chinon came into the possession of Cardinal Richelieu in the 17th c. the castle fell into decay.

Château

Opening times
1 Feb.–14 Mar.,
daily 9 a.m.–noon and
2–5 p.m.;
15 Mar.–30 June,
daily 9 a.m.–noon and
2–6 p.m.;
1 July–31 Aug., daily
9 a.m.–6 p.m.;
1–30 Sept., daily
9 a.m.–noon and 2–6 p.m.;
1 Oct.–30 Nov.,
daily 9 a.m.–noon and
2–5 p.m.

Admission charge

Château de Milieu

The château, commandingly situated on its hill, occupies an area of some 400 m (440 yd) by up to 80 m (90 yd). Of the original structure there survive mainly the circuit of walls and its numerous towers. The three parts of the complex (from E to W Fort St-Georges, the Château du Milieu and the Château du Coudray) are separated from one another by two ditches.

Approaching from the car park on the N side of the rocky plateau, we come first to the site of Fort St-Georges (to left: not open to public), which was built in the reign of Henry II Plantagenet but has now almost completely disappeared. Henry died here in 1189 and was buried at Fontevraud-l'Abbaye (see entry).

We now turn right and cross the ditch on a bridge. (For Son et lumière, see Practical Information.)

The middle section of the castle is entered by the Tour de l'Horloge (Clock Tower; 12th c.), which is 35 m (115 ft) high, 12 m (39 ft) wide but only 3 m (10 ft) deep. It now houses a small museum on the subject of Jeanne d'Arc (including children's drawings depicting her), together with the mechanism of an old clock.

From the S wall, with remains of the wall-walk, there is a fine view of the lower town and the river.

On the surviving end wall of the Grande Salle is a chimneypiece, above which is a tablet, set up in 1929, commemorating the meeting between Jeanne d'Arc and Charles VII. A door to the left leads into a small room containing a model and ground plan of the château. In the following rooms are a small-scale model of the equestrian statue of Jeanne d'Arc (by Paul Dubois) in the Place St-Augustin in Paris, a 17th c. Aubusson tapestry depicting the meeting between Jeanne and

Chinon, on the Vienne

the king, genealogical tables of the houses of Valois and Plantagenet, Gallo-Roman finds, etc.

The courtyard of the Château du Milieu is attractively planted with trees.

Beyond the second ditch (crossed by a bridge) is the Château du Coudray, the most westerly part of the castle. On the right is the Donjon (Keep), in which members of the order of Templars (accused of heresy and later dissolved by the Council of Vienne, 1312) were imprisoned in 1308. The inscriptions on the walls are ascribed to the incarcerated Templars. Jeanne d'Arc stayed on the first floor when she came to Chinon in 1429. From the S side of the tower there is a beautiful view of the river, looking downstream.

Château du Coudray

A little street (Rue de l'Echo) runs N from the château to a spot where there is a remarkable echo, reflected back from the castle walls.

Echo

Old town

The old town of Chinon lies between the foot of the castle hill and the Vienne, reached by a steep lane descending the hill. Here – particularly in Rue Voltaire – there are a number of excellently restored 15th and 16th c. houses.

In the main square of the medieval town, the Place du Grand-Carroi, is the Maison des Etats-Généraux (House of the States General), in which the States met in 1427–28. The house

House of States General

Chinon

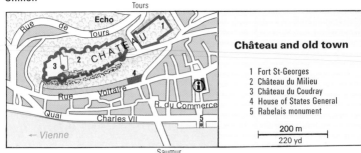

Tours

Echo

Château and old town

1 Fort St-Georges
2 Château du Milieu
3 Château du Coudray
4 House of States General
5 Rabelais monument

200 m
220 yd

← Vienne

Saumur

contains a museum with mementoes of Jeanne d'Arc. A few paces E, at the foot of the steep lane running down from the château, is a well at which Jeanne d'Arc is said to have dismounted on her arrival in Chinon in 1429.

Along Rue Voltaire to the W are other handsome old houses, including the Hôtel du Gouvernement (17th c.; picturesque courtyard), the Palais du Bailliage (15th c.; now occupied by the Hostellerie Gargantua) and the Hôtel Poirier de Beauvais (16th c.), with a small round tower.

At the E end of Rue Voltaire, to the N of the Place de l'Hôtel de Ville, is a small museum devoted to wine and the craft of the cooper.

Rabelais Monument

On Quai Jeanne d'Arc, on the banks of the Vienne, is a

Tour de l'Horloge

Street in the old town

monument to Rabelais. From the nearby bridge there is a good
view of the château and the old town.

From the Ligré-Rivière station, 6 km (4 miles) SE of Chinon, an
old-time steam train runs on summer weekends to the attractive
little town of Richelieu (1 hour's journey).

Old-time railway

Avoine

At Avoine, on the left bank of the Loire, stands the Centrale
Nucléaire d'Avoine-Chinon, the first French atomic power
station (1969), with a tall outlook tower. Visitors can see round
it by previous arrangement (parties only: apply to Centrale de
Chinon, F-37420 Avoine).

Situation
12 km (7½ miles) N

Cour-Cheverny

Region: Centre
Département: Loir-et-Cher
Altitude: 90 m (295 ft)
Population: 2000

The village of Cour-Cheverny lies some 10 km (6 miles) SE of
Blois on the little River Conon, which flows into the Beuvron,
a left-bank tributary of the Loire. SE of the village begins the
large Forêt de Cheverny, a wooded area with numerous lakes.

Situation

Château de Cheverny

The Château de Cheverny (completed in 1634) was built by
Henri Hurault on the site of an earlier building, of which part
survives in the dependences of the château. It still belongs to
the Hurault de Cheverny family.
The château is notable for its stylistic unity. On either side of the
unusually narrow central projection are the two-storey side
wings, and beyond these are large three-storey corner blocks.
Each of these three elements in the building has a different type
of roof. On the richly decorated S front are medallions containing busts of 12 Roman emperors; the N front is plainer.

Opening times
Daily 9 a.m.–noon and
2.15–6.30 p.m.

Admission charge

Son et lumière
See Practical Information

Since the château is a family home, not all the rooms are open
to visitors.
On the ground floor, to the right, are a corridor and, adjoining
this, a room with a painted timber ceiling and painted walls.
Round the room and along the corridor, at eye level, is a frieze
of scenes from "Don Quixote".
To the left of the Baroque staircase are the Grand Salon, the
Petit Salon and the Library, containing much of the original
furniture.
The Salle des Gardes (Guard Room) on the first floor contains
a large collection of arms and armour. Beyond this is the
Chambre du Roi (King's Bedroom), which is overloaded with
decoration. In the panels of the coffered ceiling are scenes from
the story of Perseus (school of Jean Mosnier, 1600–56, who
worked in Blois); five tapestries from the Paris manufactory
(Gobelins) depict the exploits of Odysseus.

Interior

Château de Cheverny, S front

Park

The original terraced layout has not survived. In the SE of the park, which has many handsome old trees, are the outbuildings and offices of the château, with kennels for the hounds used in hunting.

Close by is the Trophy Hall, with huge numbers of antlers, etc. On the wall is a modern glass mosaic with internal lighting depicting the hunt setting out.

Beauregard

Situation
8 km (5 miles) NW

To the left of the road from Cour-Cheverny to Blois (D765), in the Forêt de Russy, is the hunting lodge of Beauregard, built about 1550. It contains a gallery of 363 17th c. portraits, including many kings. On the first floor are rooms with beautiful coffered ceilings and Delft tiles. The chapel was destroyed in the 19th c.

Villesavin

Situation
10 km (6 miles) NE

From Cour-Cheverny D102 runs NE to the hamlet of Ponts-d'Arian, on the River Beuvron, on the far side of which is the 16th c. château of Villesavin. It was built by Jean Le Breton, François I's finance minister, who directed the construction of the nearby Château de Chambord (see entry). This charming little château is in the style of the Italian Renaissance, the corner towers usual in earlier buildings being replaced by elegant pavilions. The façade is patterned with pillars, volutes (spiral scrolls) and sculpture. In the courtyard is a fountain basin in Italian marble. There is an interesting collection of carriages.

Fontevraud-l'Abbaye

Region: Pays de la Loire
Département: Maine-et-Loire
Altitude: 80 m (262 ft)
Population: 2000

The little town of Fontevraud (old spelling Fontevrault) lies a short distance from the left bank of the Loire half-way between Chinon and Saumur.

Situation

**Abbey

The abbey of Fontevraud, formerly of great importance, was founded in 1099 by Robert d'Arbrissel. The Plantagenets made large donations to the order and chose the abbey as their burial place. The order was dissolved during the French Revolution, and from 1804 to 1963 the abbey was a prison. It is now a centre for conferences, concerts and exhibitions.
The entrance to the extensive precincts of the abbey is in the centre of the town, in the Place des Plantagenets. After passing a number of classical-style offices and outbuildings visitors come to the ticket-office, where the conducted tours begin.

Opening times
1 May–31 Oct., Wed.–Mon. 9 a.m.–noon and 2–6.30 p.m.;
1 Nov.–30 Apr., Wed.–Mon. 9.30 a.m.–noon and 2–4 p.m.

Conducted tours

Admission

On the W front of the large abbey church, which was consecrated in 1119, is a Romanesque doorway with figural decoration. In the gable is a later window in Flamboyant style.

Church

Abbey church   *Kitchen*

Fontevraud-l'Abbaye

Klosteranlage

1 Entrance

2 Plantagenet tombs

3 Cloître Ste-Marie

4 Chapterhouse

5 Cloître St-Benoît

6 Chapel of St-Benoît

7 Kitchen

8 Refectory

9 Chapel of St-Lazare

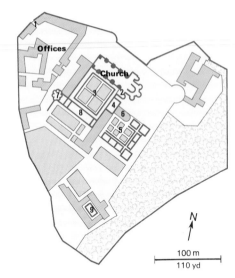

The plain, undecorated interior, without division into aisles, is of powerful spatial effect. Each bay is roofed with a spherical dome, and the church is lighted only by small windows set under the arches of the vaulting. The transept and choir are higher than the nave. The choir, unusually tall and narrow for a Romanesque church, is surrounded by ten columns and an ambulatory with three chapels (the one in the middle being slightly off the axis of the building to the right).

In the S transept are the famous Plantagenet tombs, with recumbent painted effigies: from left to right Isabella of Angoulême (wife of King John), Richard I (Cœur de Lion), Eleanor of Aquitaine (wife of Henry II) and Henry II.

Cloître Ste-Marie

In the S aisle of the church is the entrance to the Cloître Ste-Marie. Built in the 12th and 16th c., the cloister is in typical Renaissance style with the exception of the S side, which is Gothic. On its E side is the Chapterhouse, with rich figural decoration over the doorway. The vaulting is painted with frescoes (16th c.).

Cloître St-Benoît

The Cloître St-Benoît, in the style of French classicism, has only three sides, with the chapel of St-Benoît enclosing it on the N. From just outside the N side there is a good view of the apse of the abbey church.

*Kitchen

The best known part of the abbey buildings is the old Kitchen, with its striking conical roof, which stands at the SW corner of the complex. It owes its very characteristic form, however, to recent restoration.

Round the octagonal central structure are five apse-like projections, each with its own chimney hood; the main flues are in the high roof. A low door (usually closed) leads into the rib-vaulted refectory, 45 m (148 ft) long.

Near the S end of the abbey precincts stands the chapel of St-Lazare, with a small cloister. It is now used as a house of retreat.

Chapelle St-Lazare

Candes-St-Martin

The village of Candes-St-Martin lies at the outflow of the Vienne into the Loire. It takes its name from St Martin of Tours, who died here on 8 November 397. The church dedicated to him was built in the 12th–13th c., and later was fortified. The N doorway has rich figural decoration.

Situation
5 km (3 miles) N

Montsoreau

The village of Montsoreau, situated on the banks of the Loire, has a château which preserves some Gothic features but is predominantly Renaissance. The château (open Wed.–Mon. 10 a.m.–noon and 2–6 p.m.; admission charge) has been occupied since 1956 by the Musée des Goums (Moroccan troops formerly recruited into the French army).

Situation
4 km (2½ miles) N

Gerbier de Jonc

Region: Rhône-Alpes
Département: Ardèche
Altitude: 1551 m (5089 ft)

The Gerbier de Jonc and the infant Loire

Gien

Situation	The Gerbier de Jonc is a hill in the Vivarais, a region in the eastern part of the Massif Central, the natural boundary of which is formed by the Rhône valley, some 50 km (30 miles) E of the Gerbier de Jonc. At the foot of the hill are the sources of the Loire, and a short distance to the E, at a height of 1330 m (4365 ft), is the watershed between the Mediterranean and the Atlantic.
	The phonolitic (made of a volcanic rock which rings when struck) cone of the Gerbier de Jonc, with a sparse covering of vegetation, rises out of rolling upland meadows, covered in late spring with a profusion of wild narcissi, orchids and pansies. At the foot of the hill are a small car park and a restaurant. Just beside the road is one of the sources of the Loire, and there is another lower down the valley on the Ferme de la Loire. There are a number of other sources on the same groundwater horizon.
Ascent of the hill	From the car park it is a 30 minutes' climb to the summit. There is no made-up road; only steep paths, which can be hard going in wet weather. From the summit plateau, which measures some 10×20 m (11×22 yd), there is a magnificent panoramic
*View	view, extending in clear weather as far as the Alps.

Gien

Region: Centre
Département: Loiret
Altitude: 160 m (525 ft)
Population: 15,000

Situation	The little town of Gien lies on the right bank of the Loire (at this point already enclosed by an embankment), some 65 km (40 miles) SE of Orléans and 75 km (47 miles) N of Bourges. The château is conspicuously situated on higher ground. Downstream from the town is an atomic power station.

Château

Location
Place du Château

Opening times
Whitsun–31 Oct.,
daily 9–11.45 a.m. and
2.15–6.30 p.m.;
1 Nov.–Whitsun,
daily 9–11.45 a.m. and
2.15–5.30 p.m.

Admission charge

The château, a plain brick building with tall gables, was erected in 1494–1500 for Comtesse Anne de Beaujeu, daughter of Louis XI, on the site of an earlier building. From the SE tower there is a very fine view. The château now houses the Musée International de la Chasse (International Hunting Museum), with weapons and equipment of the chase and hunting trophies, as well as tapestries, pictures and ceramics on hunting themes. An unusual feature is the button collection, with great numbers of buttons depicting game, hounds, etc.

Church of Ste-Jeanne-d'Arc	NW of the château is the church of Ste-Jeanne-d'Arc, a 19th c. building restored after the Second World War.

Porcelain Manufactory

Location
Place de la Victoire

To the NW of the town, near the river, is the Porcelain Manufactory, founded in 1821.

Gien, with its château

Visitors can see round this celebrated establishment. There is a small Porcelain Museum with a sales point.

Opening times
Mon.–Fri. 9.30–11.30 a.m.
and 2–5.30 p.m.

Briare

The little town of Briare, on the right bank of the Loire, is notable for an early feat of civil engineering – the aqueduct which carries the Canal de Briare, a 17th c. waterway 56 km (35 miles) long, over the Loire.

7 km (4¼ miles) N, in Pont-Chevron, Gallo-Roman mosaics (2nd c. A.D.) have been brought to light by excavation. Here, too, there is a 19th c. château.

Situation
10 km (6 miles) SE

La Bussière

La Bussière lies in a well-wooded area with many lakes. By a lake to the N of the village is a château of the 15th and 16th c., now containing a small Fishing Museum.

Situation
12 km (7½ miles) NE

Châtillon-Coligny

Châtillon-Coligny is a road junction on the Canal de Briare (see above) and the River Loing, a left-bank tributary of the Seine. It was the birthplace of Gaspard de Coligny (1519–72), appointed Admiral of France in 1552, who played a major part in the war with Spain.

Situation
25 km (15 miles) NE

St-Fargeau

Situation
42 km (26 miles) E

The little town of St-Fargeau, on the Loing, is dominated by a large château built between the 12th and the 18th c. It also has a fine church dating from the 13th to the 15th c.

Gorges de la Loire

See Loire Gorge

La . . . and Le . . .

See under main element in name

Langeais

Region: Centre
Département: Indre-et-Loire
Altitude: 55 m (180 ft)
Population: 4000

Situation

Langeais lies on the right bank of the Loire 25 km (15 miles) W of Tours. In Roman times there was a military camp here, and the site was also of military importance in later times. In the

Château de Langeais, courtyard

10th c. Fulco Nerra, Count of Anjou, built a castle, scanty remains of which can be seen adjoining the present château. During the 12th c. it was held for a time by Richard Lionheart.

Château

The château stands on a hill beside the main road through the town. It was built in the short space of only four years (1465–69), and since then has undergone practically no alteration: hence its stylistic unity. It was built for Louis XI, and in 1491 the marriage of Charles VIII and Anne de Bretagne was celebrated here with great pomp.

The plain, uncompromising exterior and massive corner towers emphasise the defensive function of the château. The courtyard is entered by way of a large drawbridge and a passage under the gatehouse. In the passage, on right, is a tablet commemorating a former owner, Jacques Siegfried, who restored the château and in 1904 presented it to the Institut de France.

The spacious courtyard is bounded at the near end by the two wings of the château and is continued by terraced gardens rising to the ruins of the 10th c. Donjon (Keep), with the graves of Jacques Siegfried and his wife.

Thirteen rooms of the château are open to visitors. They are notable for their furniture and furnishings, including tapestries (mainly Flemish), richly ornamented chimneypieces, etc.

Location
Place du Château

Opening times
Tues.–Sun. 9 a.m.–noon and 2–6.30 p.m.
Mon. 2–6.30 p.m.

Conducted tours

Admission charge

Interior

Loches

Region: Centre
Département: Indre-et-Loire
Altitude: 70 m (230 ft)
Population: 7000

Loches, 40 km (25 miles) SE of Tours, is picturesquely situated on the slopes above the Indre, a left-bank tributary of the Loire.

Situation

*Castle hill

The old town of Loches, situated on a hill which rises commandingly above the river and surrounded by a circuit of walls 2 km (1¼ miles) long, must be seen on foot. This "town within a town" is entered by the Porte Royale, on the NW side of the walls. This imposing town gate (13th and 15th c.) was originally approached by a drawbridge. On the outside wall is a tablet commemorating a visit by Jeanne d'Arc.

Passing through the gate and turning left, we come in a few paces to the entrance to the Maison Lansyer, once the home of the landscape painter Emmanuel Lansyer (1838–93), and the inner section of the gate, which houses a regional museum (folk traditions, costumes; closed Fri.).

At the upper end of the street is the church of St-Ours (dedicated to the town's patron saint), which was founded in 962 but in its present from is mainly 12th c. In the porch is a

Church of St-Ours

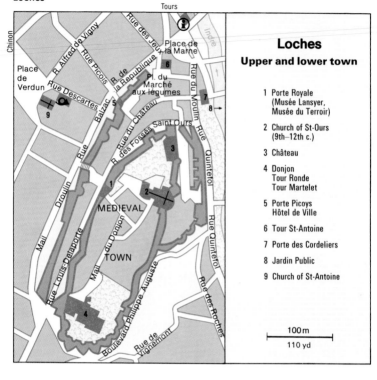

Tours

Loches

Upper and lower town

1 Porte Royale
(Musée Lansyer,
Musée du Terroir)

2 Church of St-Ours
(9th–12th c.)

3 Château

4 Donjon
Tour Ronde
Tour Martelet

5 Porte Picoys
Hôtel de Ville

6 Tour St-Antoine

7 Porte des Cordeliers

8 Jardin Public

9 Church of St-Antoine

100 m

110 yd

Romanesque doorway with rich figural decoration. Just inside
the door is a Roman altar with relief ornament, now used as a
holy water stoup.
The nave is roofed with sharply pointed pyramidal steeples
which give the church its very characteristic silhouette.

Château

Just to the left of the W front of the church is the entrance to the
old royal castle (15th–16th c.), the residence of Charles VII and
his successors. In the interior (open 9 a.m.–noon and 2–6 p.m.;
admission charge), visitors come first to the Salle Charles VII,
beyond which is the Salle Jeanne d'Arc, with a small collection
of weapons and a number of tapestries. Then follows a room
containing the beautiful alabaster tomb of Agnès Sorel (c.
1422–50), Charles VII's favourite. In the fourth room is a
famous triptych of 1485 (school of Tours) from the Charterhouse of Le Liget (see p. 82). The sequence of rooms ends with
the Oratory of Anne de Bretagne and its antechamber.
To the right of the entrance to the château a short flight of steps
leads down to the Tour d'Agnès Sorel. Passing under this
tower, we come on to a terrace commanding extensive views.
Prominent features in the lower town are the Tour St-Antoine
with its Renaissance helm roof and, to the right of this, the Porte
des Cordeliers.

Returning past the church of St-Ours and continuing S, we reach the Donjon or Keep (open 9.30 a.m.–12.15 p.m. and 2.30–6.15 p.m.; admission charge), which together with its subsidiary buildings occupies the southern tip of the upper town. Built in the 11th c., this large and forbidding structure was used for centuries, from 1249 onwards, as a state prison. The intermediate floors have now disappeared, but a steep and at some points very narrow staircase (not recommended for visitors subject to vertigo) runs up inside and sometimes within the walls to their highest point. The platform at the top is cramped, with an area of only 3 sq. m (30 sq. ft), but offers fine views in all directions.

In the 15th c. further defensive structures were built on to the Donjon, including the Tour Ronde (to the W), with a number of prison cells, and the Tour du Martelet, also containing dungeons, in one of which Lodovico Sforza, Duke of Milan, spent the rest of his life after being captured in the battle of Novara (1500). In the cells are inscriptions cut by prisoners, as well as Stations of the Cross and an altar hewn from the stone of the walls.

Visitors on a conducted tour can pass through the walls at the Donjon and walk round outside the circuit. Otherwise it is necessary to return from here to the Porte Royale.

Donjon (Keep)

Lower town

The most picturesque parts of the lower town lie N and W of the castle hill. The old streets and lanes have preserved the aspect of a quiet little provincial town.

Church of St-Ours

Porte des Cordeliers

Town Hall	The Hôtel de Ville (Town Hall), a charming Renaissance building erected between 1535 and 1543, stands near the Porte Picoys, one of the old town gates, in a style transitional between Gothic and Renaissance.
Tour St-Antoine	Turning right from the Town Hall through the old town, we see the Tour St-Antoine (1529), all that is left of a 16th c. church.
Porte des Cordeliers	The Porte des Cordeliers is another of the four town gates which afforded passage through the walls of the lower town. Outside the gate a bridge crosses the Indre to the Jardin Public (Public Gardens), from which there is a view of the town and the château.

Beaulieu

Situation
1 km (¾ mile) E

Beaulieu, an outlying part of Loches, has the remains of an abbey founded c. 1000, with a handsome tower. The church of St-Laurent also has a Romanesque tower.

Le Liget

Situation
10 km (6 miles) E

The Charterhouse of Le Liget (Chartreuse du Liget) lies in a sequestered position in the Forêt de Loches. Tradition has it that the monastery was founded by Henry II of England in penitence for the murder of Thomas Becket in 1170.
Within the extensive precincts of the monastery, enclosed by a wall, are a 12th c. chapel and an 18th c. cloister.
1 km (¾ mile) E is the 12th c. chapel of La Corroirie, which also belonged to the Charterhouse.

Montrésor

Situation
17 km (10½ miles) E

The village of Montrésor lies on the Indrois, a right-bank tributary of the Indre. It has a fortified Renaissance château built on the site of an earlier castle belonging to Fulco Nerra; it contains furniture and pictures by Polish artists.
In the fine village church (1520–41) is the 16th c. tomb of the Bastarnay family.

Loire Gorge (Gorges de la Loire)

Region: Rhône-Alpes
Départements: Ardèche and Haute-Loire

In its upper reaches, between its source on the Gerbier de Jonc (see entry) and the town of Le Puy (see entry), the Loire flows through a varied and very beautiful upland region of dense forests and great expanses of hill grazing, covered in early summer with multitudes of narcissi and orchids.

Porte Picoys and Hôtel de Ville, Loches ▶

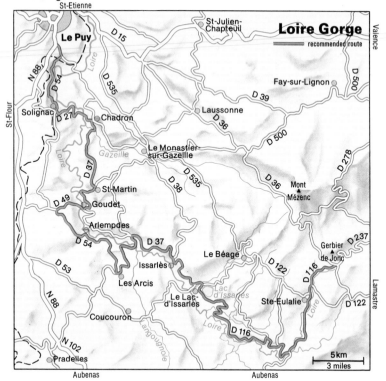

Loire Gorge

━━━━ recommended route

*Through the Loire Gorge

Length
c. 100 km (60 miles)

Time required
c. 6 hours

From the Gerbier de Jonc take D116, southward alongside the infant Loire, with fine rearward views of the hill. The road then runs through a range of rounded hills, at some points passing high above the deeply indented bed of the river.

Lac d'Issarlès

The road (D116) now passes the Lac d'Issarlès, an almost circular lake surrounded by forest. There is a good view of the lake from the village of Le Lac d'Issarlès, a little holiday resort with a beach of fine sand shaded by pines.

Arlempdes

Farther downstream we come by way of D116, D37 and D54 to Arlempdes, with a ruined castle (12th–15th c.) on a crag of volcanic origin. There is an impressive view into the river valley. The little town at the foot of the hill has a fine church and an 11th c. gate in the old town walls.

Beaufort

10 km (6 miles) N of Arlempdes is the village of Goudet, beautifully situated at the mouths of two narrow valleys. It is a popular summer resort with French holidaymakers. On the hill

The Lac d'Issarlès, in a tranquil holiday region

above the village, still partly ringed with walls, is the ruined castle of Beaufort.

St-Martin lies high above the right bank of the Loire, with a view of the Velay hills and the Le Puy basin.
From here the route continues via Chadron and Solignac to join the *route nationale* (N88) which leads N to Le Puy.

St-Martin-de-Fugères

Moulins

Region: Auvergne
Département: Allier
Altitude: 220 m (722 ft)
Population: 27,000

Moulins, chief town of the département of Allier, lies in the upper valley of the Allier, a left-bank tributary of the Loire, into which it flows at Nevers, some 50 km (30 miles) N. To the S of the town rises the Massif Central.

Situation

The town, which grew up around a castle in the 10th c., owes its name to the numerous mills once driven by the waters of the Allier. In 1327 Moulins became the capital of the region of Bourbonnais, created a duchy by Louis I. In the reign of François I the duchy of Bourbon was annexed to the crown.

History

Place de l'Hôtel-de-Ville

The Place de l'Hôtel-de-Ville lies in the centre of the picturesque older part of the town. On the N side of the square are the Office du Tourisme and the Hôtel de Ville.

Tour de l'Horloge (Clock Tower)

At the W end of the square stands the Tour de l'Horloge (Clock Tower) or Beffroi (Belfry) of 1455, a massive rectangular structure topped by a balustraded gallery, above which is a lantern with a *jacquemart* or "Jack of the clock" (mechanical figures which strike the hours and quarters).

Folk Museum

Location
Place de l'Ancien-Palais

Opening times
Daily 10 a.m.–noon and 3–6 p.m.

Admission charge

The Musée du Folklore et du Vieux Moulins, housed in a 15th c. mansion, displays in its 15 rooms a wide range of material of local interest, including old craft implements (large collection of irons), a model of a peasant house, costumes, furniture, dolls and material on the local milling trade.

Cathédrale Notre-Dame

Location
Square Laussedat

A little way N of the Place de l'Hôtel-de-Ville is the Cathédrale Notre-Dame, originally a collegiate church but raised to cathedral status in 1823. The choir, in Flamboyant style, dates from the original late 15th c. church, and has fine 15th and 16th c. stained glass in the ambulatory. The nave with its twin spires (95 m – 312 ft high) is neo-Gothic of the late 19th c.

Treasury

The Cathedral treasury, in the sacristy, contains works of religious art, including the famous triptych by the Master of Moulins (late 15th c.).

Pavillon d'Anne de Beaujeu

Location
Square Laussedat

Opening times
Temporarily closed

Facing the Cathedral, to the NW, is the arcaded Pavillon d'Anne de Beaujeu (*c.* 1500), which, like the old keep known as the Tour Mal Coiffée, was part of the old ducal castle. It now houses the Musée d'Art et d'Archéologie, with prehistoric and Gallo-Roman material from local excavations, scuplture, pictures, faience, weapons, etc.

Mausoleum of Henri de Montmorency

Location
Rue de Paris

The Mausoleum of Duke Henri II de Montmorency is in the chapel of the Lycée Banville, to the N of the Cathedral. Henri was beheaded in 1632 for his part in a rebellion against Richelieu; the tomb, commissioned by his widow, who had been exiled to Moulins, was the work of F. Angier (*c.* 1650).

Nantes

Region: Pays de la Loire
Département: Loire-Atlantique
Altitude: 10 m (33 ft)
Population: 265,000

The old Breton port of Nantes, now chief town of the
département of Loire-Atlantique, a university town and the see
of a bishop, lies on both banks of the Loire, here divided into
several arms. The river is navigable from Nantes to its mouth, 55
km (35 miles) away. The Erdre here flows into the Loire from
the N, the final section of its course being covered over (trips by
excursion boats).

Situation

In Gallo-Roman times the town was known as Condevincum
or Civitas Namnetum. About 850 it was captured by the
Bretons, and it later became the residence of the Dukes of
Brittany. In 1532 the duchy passed to the French crown.
On 13 April 1598 Henri IV signed the Edict of Nantes, which
ended the Huguenot wars. Although the Edict confirmed the
status of Catholicism as the national religion it granted
members of the Reformed faith freedom of conscience and,
within limits, freedom to practise their religion.
Thanks to its harbour Nantes developed during the 16th c. into
a wealthy commercial town, the prosperity of which depended
from the mid 17th c. on the lively slave trade with French
possessions in the Caribbean.
Nantes became notorious during the French Revolution for the
"noyades de Nantes", when Jean-Baptiste Carrier, a member
of the National Convention, ordered the mass drowning of
opponents of the revolutionary regime in the Loire. Soon
afterwards he himself was denounced, condemned to death
and guillotined for these acts of terrorism.
In the 19th c. the importance of Nantes as a port declined
sharply, since the ocean-going ships were steadily becoming
larger and could not negotiate the lower course of the Loire.
Nowadays vessels of considerable draught use the outer
harbour of St-Nazaire (see entry).
Present-day Nantes is largely a town of modern aspect, with
many new buildings.

History

*Château Ducal

The imposing Château Ducal, surrounded by a moat which is
now partly laid out as a park, stands at the eastern end of the old
town on the Cours Kennedy, a through route carrying heavy
traffic. The original castle of the Dukes of Brittany was founded
in the 10th c.; it was rebuilt in 1466 and again enlarged in the
16th c. The Edict of Nantes was signed here.
Crossing the W side of the moat on a wide paved bridge, we
come into the block known as the Grand Gouvernement. In the
entrance passage, on right, is the ticket office, and beyond this
is a vaulted room with a tablet commemorating Anne de
Bretagne, who was born here in 1477.

Location
Cours J.–F.–Kennedy
Rue des Etats

Opening times
Wed.–Mon. 10 a.m.–noon
and 2–6 p.m.

Admission charge
(for museums)

Near the gateway leading into the courtyard is a handsome Late
Gothic seven-bucket well. From the wall on the S side of the

Courtyard

Within the Château Ducal, Nantes

courtyard, beside the Petit Gouvernement, there is a good general view of the château and the Cathedral to the N. On the wall, below the wall-walk, is a large tablet commemorating the union of Brittany with France (1532), and to the left of this a smaller one commemorating the Edict of Nantes (1598).

In the courtyard are the excavated remains of older buildings and a number of old cannon.

Museums

On the first floor of the entrance wing (the Grand Gouvernement) is the Musée d'Art Populaire Régional (Museum of Regional Folk Art), on the second floor the Musée de Ferronnerie et Céramique (Museum of Wrought Ironwork and Ceramics).

Nantes

Château Ducal

The Original Castle of the Dukes of Brittany

1 Entrance
2 Tour du Pied de Biche
3 Tour de la Boulangerie
4 Grand Gouvernement (Musée d'Art Populaire Régional, Musée de Ferronnerie et Céramique)
5 Tour de la Couronne d'Or
6 Tour des Jacobins
7 Well
8 Grand Logis
9 Tour du Port
10 Petit Gouvernement
11 Tour de la Rivière
12 Musée des Salorges
13 Tour du Fer à Cheval
14 Remains of original castle
15 Loge du Concierge
16 Vieux Donjon
17 Bastion Mercœur
18 Tour au Duc
19 Vieux Logis
20 Chapel
21 Tour des Espagnols

At the E end of the château is the Musée des Salorges, also known as the Musée de la Marine (Shipping Museum).

Cathédrale St-Pierre-et-St-Paul

To the N of the château stands the Catheral, dedicated to SS. Peter and Paul, built in the 15th c. on a site which had been occupied by several earlier churches. The crypt formed part of one of these churches.
The construction of the Cathedral continued into the second half of the 17th c. During the French Revolution it suffered much damage, and thereafter restoration work went on until 1891.

Location
Place St-Pierre

The W front overlooks Place St-Pierre, which is surrounded by the uniform façades of late 19th c. buildings. The figural decoration on the main doorway suffered severely during the Revolution; the statue of St Peter dates from 1819.
Next to the N transept, in Place du Maréchal-Foch (column in honour of Louis XVI, 1790), is a Late Gothic doorway, the Porte St-Pierre. Outside the E end of the Cathedral are the excavated remains of an earlier church.

Exterior

The interior of the Cathedral is heavily restored. The nave is considerably higher than its flanking aisles, which are lined with chapels. E of the transept a wooden partition erected during constructional work shuts off the apse and the entrance to the crypt.
In the N transept can be seen the elaborate empty tomb of General Lamoricière (1806–65). The S transept has two large stained-glass windows of 1959 in the end wall. Here, too, is the beautiful tomb, in black and white marble, of François II (Duke of Brittany, d. 1488), and in the floor close by the tomb of Françoise de Dinant (1436–99). A tablet on the wall commemorates British soldiers who fell in France in the First World War.

Interior

*Museum of Fine Art

A little way NE of the Cathedral is the Musée des Beaux-Arts (Museum of Fine Art), one of France's leading provincial museums. Of particular importance is its collection of pictures from the 13th c. onwards, mainly by Italian, Dutch, Flemish and French artists. It also has notable collections of 19th c. and contemporary art.

Location
Rue Georges-Clemenceau

Opening times
Wed.–Mon. 9.15 a.m.–noon and 1–6 p.m.

Admission charge

Archaeological Museum

Some distance from the town centre to the SW stands the Palais Dobrée, built by a 19th c. collector, which now houses the Archaeological Museum, with a large collection of material recovered by excavation in the region, ranging in date from prehistoric to Gallo-Roman times. Some items also come from churches and secular buildings destroyed during the 19th c. Other sections are devoted to the French Revolution, ethnography (America, Oceania) and Egyptian antiquities.

Location
Place Jean-V

Opening times
Wed.–Mon. 10 a.m.–noon and 2–6 p.m.

Admission charge

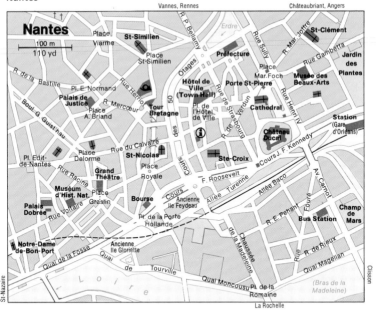

Musée Thomas Dobrée

In the same building is the Musée Dobrée, with illuminated manuscripts, incunabula, first editions, prints and pictures.

Natural History Museum

Location
Rue Voltaire

Opening times
Tues.–Sat. 10 a.m.–noon and 2–6 p.m.,
Sun. 2–6 p.m.

Admission charge

The Muséum d'Histoire Naturelle (Natural History Museum) is a short distance E of the Archaeological Museum. Recently completely renovated, it has departments of zoology, comparative anatomy, mineralogy, ethnography, etc. There is a vivarium with live reptiles and insects.
Attached to the museum is a specialised library of some 20,000 volumes (open to the public).

Jules Verne Museum

Location
Rue de l'Hermitage

Opening times
Wed.–Mon. 10–12.30 a.m. and 2–5 p.m.

Admission charge

Planetarium

This museum devoted to Nantes' world-famous son Jules Verne (1828–1905) lies near the river harbour to the SW of the city. It contains objects which belonged to Jules Vernes, models and drawings illustrating his novels – forerunners of our modern science fiction – and contemporary editions of his works.

The Planetarium adjoining the Jules Verne Museum was opened in 1981. It has equipment enabling practically all possible constellations to be projected on to the inner surface of its hemispherical dome.

Ancenis

The little town of Ancenis is beautifully situated above the right
bank of the Loire. It once had a busy river harbour, but its
economy is now largely centred on the trade in agricultural
produce (wine, beef cattle). It has numbers of old houses and
a château built by the Dukes of Brittany in the 15th and 16th c.

Situation
41 km (25 miles) NE

Champtoceaux

Champtoceaux, on the left bank of the Loire, has a fine church
and the ruins of a medieval castle.
On the other side of the Loire, in Oudon, is an old keep dating
from about 1400.

Situation
31 km (20 miles) NE

River Erdre

On the lower reaches of the River Erdre, which flows into the
Loire at Nantes, coming from the N, excursion boats ply
throughout the year (trips during the day and evening cruises,
sometimes with entertainments and dancing). Along the river
are a series of elegant châteaux and manor-houses, including
the Château de la Gacherie (16th c.) on the W bank. The Boats
go as far as the Plaine de Mazerolles (12 km – $7\frac{1}{2}$ miles), where
the river becomes much wider; the trip takes about 4 hours.
Departures from 24 Quai de Versailles, Nantes (parking
facilities).

Boat trips

Nevers

Region: Bourgogne
Département: Nièvre
Altitude: 185 m (610 ft)
Population: 50,000

Nevers, chief town of the old Nivernais region and now of the
département of Nièvre, lies on rising ground above the right
bank of the Loire, here joined by the River Nièvre flowing down
from the N. Here the Loire begins the wide bend which
continues by way of Orléans to Blois.
Visitors approaching the middle valley of the Loire, the "garden
of France", from the E normally make their first contact with the
river here.

Situation

Originally founded by Celts, the town became in Roman times
the important military base of Noviodunum Aeduorum, from
which Caesar's troops advanced in 52 B.C. against the Gallic
stronghold of Gergovia (near Clermont-Ferrand), to be
repulsed by Vercingetorix's Gauls.
From the 16th c. Nevers rose to considerable prosperity
through the manufacture of faience – an industry which still
makes a contribution to the town's economy.

History

Nevers, gateway to the "garden of France"

Ducal Palace, Nevers

Ducal Palace

The Palais Ducal (Ducal Palace), a fine example of Renaissance secular architecture, stands at the N end of a small public garden which extends to the edge of a steep scarp falling down towards the river (view). The palace was built in the 15th and 16th c. The façade facing the Loire is dominated by the central staircase tower, with relief decoration between the windows, and an octagonal tower at either end. On the left-hand tower is a tablet commemorating Louise-Marie de Gonzague and Marie de la Grange d'Arquian, two princesses of Nevers who became queens of Poland. The dormer windows are flanked alternately by columns and by caryatids.
The palace is not open to the public.

Location
Place Ducale

Cathedral

The Cathédrale St-Cyr-et-Ste-Juliette stands diagonally opposite the Ducal Palace, on a site which was occupied by a church as early as the 4th c. The church was several times enlarged and rebuilt between the 4th and the 12th c.; then in 1221 most of it was destroyed by fire. The present building shows the styles of various periods between the 13th and 17th c. It is one of the few churches in France with two choirs.

Location
Place Ducale

Although most of the building dates from the Gothic period, it lacks the vertical thrust characteristic of Gothic: the nave has an effect of breadth and massiveness, in spite of the large windows which take up much of the wall area.
The W front is Romanesque, with much 19th c. restoration, particularly in the upper part. The richly decorated S tower, flat-topped, is 52m (171 ft) high; from the top there are fine panoramic views.

Exterior

The entrance to the Cathedral is in the N transept. The nave, fully 100 m (330 ft) long, was rebuilt in the 14th c., as were the choir and choir chapels at the E end after a further fire. The position of the oldest parts of the building indicate that the original church, contrary to usual practice, was oriented to the W.
During the restoration of war damage after the last war a number of 12th c. graves and an Early Christian baptistery (not open to the public) were discovered under the Gothic E choir. The Romanesque choir, raised above the level of the nave, has remains of a 12th c. fresco of Christ in a mandorla (aureole), surrounded by the symbols of the Evangelists. In the crypt under this choir, closed by a grille, is an early 16th c. Entombment of painted stone.
In the S transept are a doorway with sculptural decoration and a Renaissance spiral staircase with an openwork stone cage.

Interior

Porte du Croux

The imposing Porte du Croux (14th c.), the only one of the old town gates to survive, is a short distance W of the Cathedral. The moat, now filled in, was crossed by a double drawbridge, the mechanism of which was housed in the gateway (the recesses in the wall for the levers which operated it can still be seen).

Location
Promenade des Remparts

The Musée Archéologique in the Porte du Croux (open in summer 2–6 p.m.; admission charge) contains ancient and Romanesque sculpture.

From here there is a rewarding walk alongside the old town walls to the street flanking the river.

Faience Museum

In Rue St-Genest, to the S of the gate, is the Faience Museum (open Wed.–Mon. 10 a.m.–noon and 2–6 p.m.; admission charge), with a large collection of ceramics, enamels and glass.

Place Carnot

Place Carnot, on the N side of the old town, is the busiest street intersection in the city centre. NW of the square lies the beautiful Parc Municipal.

Chapelle Ste-Marie

Just E of the square stands the Chapelle Ste-Marie, built about 1640 in Italian High Baroque style. Now deconsecrated, it houses periodic art exhibitions.

Couvent St-Gildard

Location
Rue de Lourdes

Opening times
Daily 7.30 a.m.–7 p.m.
(chapel only)

The Convent of St-Gildard, occupied by the Congrégation des Sœurs de Nevers (founded 1680), lies near the NW corner of the municipal park. Marie-Bernarde Soubirous, better known as Bernadette (canonised 1933), who had visions of the Virgin in her native Pyrenean town of Lourdes, entered the convent in 1866 and died there on 16 April 1879. Her glass sarcophagus in the chapel of the convent draws many thousands of pilgrims.

*Church of St-Etienne

Location
Rue St-Etienne

The church of St-Etienne (St Stephen's) is in the NE of the old town. This purely Romanesque church, consecrated in 1097, is one of the most notable monuments of the past in Nevers. Its architecture shows some affinities with the Romanesque of Auvergne.

Some remains of the original porch have been preserved. The interior, on three levels, is surprisingly light. In the choir, which is surrounded by three chapels, three Merovingian sarcophagi have recently been exposed.

Faience manufactories

The town's oldest manufactory, the Faiencerie Montagnon (established 1648), is near the Porte du Croux.

To the N of the town are the firms of Bernard, in Avenue Colbert, and E. Georges, in Rue Bovet. Visitors can see round the factories.

Decize

Situation
34 km (21 miles) SE

The ancient little town of Decize (pop. 7000) lies at the junction of the Aron with the Loire and at the S end of the 174 km (108 mile) long Canal du Nivernais, which links the Loire

with the Yonne. The Canal Latéral à la Loire runs just S of the town.
Above Decize rises an old castle of the Counts of Nevers. It has a notable church (St-Aré) with a crypt which is believed to be Merovingian.

The Canal du Nivernais offers attractive scope for cruising. Boats can be hired in Decize (see Practical Information, Cruising on rivers and canals).

Canal cruising

Noirmoutier

Region: Pays de la Loire
Département: Vendée
Area: 48 sq. km (18½ sq. miles)

The island of Noirmoutier, just under 20 km (12½ miles) long and up to 7 km (4½ miles) wide, lies off the French Atlantic coast some 40 km (25 miles) S of the Loire estuary. It extends along the S side of the Baie de Bourgneuf, on the N side of which is the seaside resort of Pornic (see St-Nazaire).

Situation

From the road junction at Beauvoir-sur-Mer D22 runs SW to the villages of La Barre-de-Monts and Fromentine, from which a road bridge (toll) opened in 1971 crosses the mud-flats to the southern tip of the island.

Road bridge

An interesting alternative approach to the island is by the 4·15 km (2½ mile) long Passage du Gois, a paved causeway constructed in the 19th c. which is covered by several metres of water at high tide and is passable for a period of 2–3 hours at low tide. On the approach roads are boards showing the possible times of crossing, which change from day to day. At intervals along the causeway are timber platforms which provide a refuge for travellers caught by the tide. It is inadvisable to linger on the mud-flats.
At the near end of the Passage du Gois is a restaurant (oysters).

*Passage du Gois

The island of Noirmoutier is predominantly flat and sandy. Pinewoods of any considerable extent are found mainly in the northern part. The best sandy beaches are on the W side, facing the open sea. A contribution to the island's economy is made by the large salt-pans, from which salt is won by the gradual evaporation of sea water. The extensive shallows which are exposed at low tide are used for the cultivation of mussels and oysters. The early vegetables grown on the island are much esteemed. There is also a lively tourist and holiday trade, particularly in the height of summer.

The island

Noirmoutier-en-l'Ile

The chief place, Noirmoutier-en-l'Ile, lies in the broader northern part of the island, which is traversed by a road with dual carriageway. S and W of the little town are salt-pans, and

Noirmoutier

Noirmoutier-en-l'Île . . .

. . . and its castle

to the N is a wooded area, the Bois de la Chaize, with many holiday houses.

The town centre lies off the busy main road. There is an attractive pedestrian precinct with many restaurants, boutiques and other shops.

Church of St-Philibert

The church of St-Philibert, to the E of the pedestrian zone, preserves some Romanesque work (9th–11th, 14th and 17th c.). The massive tower was built in 1875, replacing an earlier wooden tower which was destroyed by fire.

Hanging from the roof of the nave is a model of a 50-gun frigate of 1802.

The church has a very fine 12th c. crypt, rediscovered only in the 19th c. Measuring 8.50 by 6 m (28 by 20 ft), with a vaulted roof, it contains the so-called "Tomb of St Philibert" (11th c.).

Château

Opposite the church is the château (open Wed.–Mon. 10 a.m.–noon and 2.30–5.30 p.m.; admission charge), a sturdy little fortified castle which dates in part from the 12th c. There is a rewarding circuit of the wall-walk. The keep, with residential apartments, contains a small museum (minerals, stuffed birds, naval history, English china). From the roof there are beautiful views, particularly to the S and E, over the little harbour and the salt-pans.

Aquarium

By the harbour on the canal is a recently opened Aquarium, with a large number of glass-fronted tanks and pools containing sea creatures from the surrounding waters.

Jeanne d'Arc . . .

. . . omnipresent in Orléans

Orléans

Region: Centre
Département: Loiret
Altitude: 110 m (361 ft)
Population: 110,000

Orléans, chief town of the Centre region and the département of Loiret, an episcopal see and a university town, lies on the middle course of the Loire, at the most northerly point in the river's wide bend. It is a pleasant town, finely laid out, and a good base from which to visit the châteaux of the Loire. To the NE extends the Forêt d'Orléans.

Situation

Orléans occupies the site of the Gallic Cenabum, which was destroyed by Caesar in 52 B.C. From the 3rd c. onwards it appears in the records as an important road junction, under the name of Aurelianum. In 451 the town was besieged by Attila and then relieved by the resolute Bishop Aignan (later canonised); in 498 it was taken by Clovis I, king of the Franks. During the Hundred Years War, in 1428–29, Orléans was the last stronghold of the French, under siege by English forces. Jeanne d'Arc, the "Maid of Orléans", who had been received by Charles VII at Chinon (see entry) on 25 February 1429, accompanied the relieving French army which freed the town on 8 May – a turning-point in the war with England. During the Wars of Religion Orléans was a Huguenot stronghold.

History

*Place du Martroi

The spacious Place du Martroi is the main square of the old town, which is now ringed by broad boulevards. The name of the square comes from the Latin *martyretum*, an early Christian cemetery. In the centre of the square stands an equestrian statue of Jeanne d'Arc (1855), with reliefs on the base depicting scenes from her life.

Cathedral

Location
Place Ste-Croix

Opening times
Closed noon–2 p.m.

The imposing Cathédrale Ste-Croix (Cathedral of the Holy Cross) stands to the E of the Place du Martroi, approached by Rue Royale and Rue Jeanne d'Arc. It was built from 1278 onwards on the site of an earlier 10th c. church, of which some foundations survive. Work on the construction of the Cathedral, which is mainly in High to Late Gothic style, was frequently interrupted and continued into the 16th c. During the Wars of Religion the piers supporting the crossing were blown up by the troops of the Prince de Condé, setting fire to the rest of the Cathedral, then still unfinished. The subsequent rebuilding (17th–18th c.) followed the original Gothic model. The whole church was thoroughly restored in the early 19th c.

Exterior

Outside the W front are two stones with modern reliefs depicting (left) the vision of Jeanne d'Arc and (right) her death at the stake. The stones serve as bases for flagstaffs.
The façade of the Cathedral is flanked by two identical flat-topped towers. The three doorways, with tall pointed arches,

The Cathedral, at the end of Rue Jeanne d'Arc

are relatively narrow. The sculptural decoration is predominantly Flamboyant, with some Renaissance features. The figural sculpture between the doorways is Baroque, as are the cartouche, borne by two angels, above the central doorway and the tympanums of the side doorways.

Outside the N transept the excavations at present in progress have brought to light the foundations of a round tower. The doorway in the S transept is a work of the High Renaissance. The nave, transept and choir have richly articulated Gothic buttresses; unusual gargoyles as water-spouts. Over the crossing is a slender spire.

Much of the interior decoration, including the stained glass in the nave and some works of sculpture in the choir, dates from the 19th c. Fine 18th c. carved choir-stalls.

The choir, crypt and treasury can be seen only on a conducted tour.

Interior

Old Town Hall

To the NW of the Cathedral is the Ancien Hôtel de Ville (Old Town Hall), a beautiful Renaissance building of 1530 in stone and brick. François II, who had come to Orléans to open a meeting of the States General, died here in 1560.

In front of the double stone staircase in the centre of the façade is a bronze statue of Jeanne d'Arc (19th c.).

On the ground floor of the right-hand wing is a branch of the Office de Tourisme.

Location
Place de l'Etape

Old Town Hall

New Town Hall

The classical-style New Town Hall stands opposite the old one on the other side of the street.

Museum of Fine Art

Location
Place de la République

The Musée des Beaux-Arts (Museum of Fine Art; open daily in summer 10 a.m.–noon and 2–6 p.m. in winter 10 a.m.–noon and 2–5 p.m.; admission charge) is housed in the Hôtel des Créneaux (to the S of Rue Jeanne d'Arc), which was the Town Hall from the 15th c. to the French Revolution. The museum has a rich collection of French painting of the 16th–19th c., a print room and examples of modern sculpture.

Historical and
Archaeological Museum

Immediately W of the Museum of Fine Art is the Musée Historique et Archéologique (Historical and Archaeological Museum). Mainly devoted to the Gallo-Roman and medieval periods, it also has locally produced ceramics and a collection of popular prints.

Old town

To the S of the two museums is a charming old quarter with fine Renaissance houses, notable among them the Maison de la Coquille and the Maison d'Alibert.

Church of St-Paul

Location
Rue du Cheval-Rouge

The church of St-Paul, to the S of the Place du Martroi, dates from the 15th c. but was almost completely destroyed during the Second World War. The only surviving parts are the façade and a chapel (enlarged in the 17th c.) containing a 16th c. Black Virgin.

Church of Notre-Dame de Recouvrance

Location
Rue Notre-Dame-de-
Recouvrance

The 16th c. church of Notre-Dame de Recouvrance, to the S of St-Paul, has Renaissance sculpture over the high altar and a beautiful 16th c. stained-glass window.
In the vicinity are a number of well-preserved Renaissance houses.

Church of St-Aignan

Location
Rue Neuve St-Aignan

In the SE of the old town, near the Loire, is the church of St-Aignan, dedicated to the valiant bishop of Orléans (358–453) who defended the town against Attila's hordes in 451. Following repeated destruction there survive only the transept and the beautiful Late Gothic choir (15th–16th c.). Under the choir is the crypt (completed 1029), one of the earliest and largest vaulted hall-crypts in France.

Parc de la Source

Location
7 km (4½ miles) S of the
Loire, in the outlying district
of La Source

The Parc de la Source contains the source of the Loiret, a left-bank tributary of the Loire, which has a course of only 12 km (7½ miles); it is in fact a resurgence of the Loire. A number of flower shows are held annually in the park.

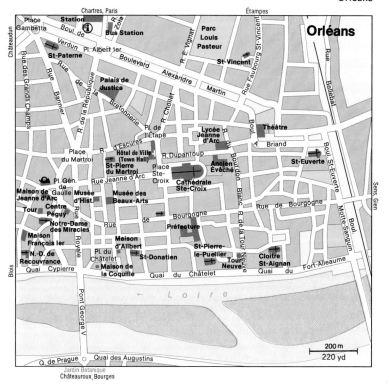

Orléans

Bellegarde-du-Loiret

Bellegarde-du-Loiret, chief town of a canton, lies in a fertile agricultural area. It has a château with a 14th c. keep and a Romanesque church (beautiful doorway with figured capitals; 17th c. pictures in interior).

Situation
48 km (30 miles) E

Cléry-St-André

Cléry-St-André lies a few kilometres from the left bank of the Loire on its tributary the Ardoux. The Gothic church of Notre-Dame (15th c.) contains the tomb of Louis XI (1423–83); the 17th c. marble statue of the king replaces the original bronze figure which was removed and melted down by the Huguenots. In the royal vault rest the remains of Louis XI and his second wife Charlotte of Savoy. A notable feature of the church is the richly decorated Renaissance Chapelle St-Jacques in the S aisle.

Situation
15 km (9 miles) SW

Paray-le-Monial

Region: Bourgogne
Département: Saône-et-Loire
Altitude: 245 m (804 ft)
Population: 12,000

Situation

The little Burgundian town of Paray-le-Monial, a notable pilgrimage centre, lies in the upper Loire valley between Roanne and Moulins, some kilometres from the river. Through the centre of the town flows the Bourbince, accompanied by the southern part of the 114 km (71 mile) long Canal du Centre (linking the Loire with the Saône). The famous Charolais beef cattle are reared in the surrounding area.

History

Founded in 973 as a Benedictine house, Paray-le-Monial claims to have been the place of origin of the worship of the Sacred Heart in France, based on the visions of the nun (later canonised) Marguerite-Marie Alacoque (1647–90), who lived in the Monastère de la Visitation here. Fostered by successive Popes, the worship of the Sacred Heart spread throughout the whole Catholic world in the 19th c.

* Basilique du Sacré-Cœur

Location
Rue des Ecoles

The church of the Sacred Heart (Basilique du Sacré-Cœur), on the right bank of the Bourbince, was built in the 12th c. on the model of the abbey church of Cluny, the largest benedictine house in France. It is one of the finest and most appealing Romanesque churches in Burgundy.

Exterior

The end facing the river has three round-arched doorways, and within the porch are two piers with figured capitals. Above the side doorways are two square towers with helm roofs, and over the crossing is a massive octagonal tower (rebuilt in 19th c.) which dominates the whole church. To the right of the façade are the conventual buildings, in classical style.
Passing to the left of the church, we come to the beautiful and clearly articulated Romanesque apse; the chapel in the S transept is Gothic. Here, too, is the entrance to the park (see below).

Interior

The nave, which is surprisingly high (22 m – 72 ft), and lateral aisles are vaulted with the first intimations of pointed arches. The interior, sparsely decorated, is of powerful spatial effect. Round the choir runs an ambulatory, with three chapels, and in the dome of the apse are remains of a 14th c. fresco depicting Christ in a mandorla.

Park

To the E of the church is the Parc des Chapelains, shaded by fine old trees. In a small building to the left of the park gate are a collection of mementoes of Marguerite-Marie Alacoque and a reconstitution of her convent cell.

Basilique du Sacré-Cœur, Paray-le-Monial ▶

In the park is an altar surmounted by a dome in 19th c. neo-Romanesque/Byzantine style, with benches set out in the open air in front of it. Also within the park are a number of grottoes of the Virgin, and round the enclosing walls are modern Stations of the Cross. On the S side of the park is a hospice for pilgrims.

Diorama

Against the W wall of the park, to the left of the gate, a Diorama (admission charge), with 17 scenes, depicts the life of Ste Marguerite-Marie Alacoque and the development of the cult of the Sacred Heart.

Chapelle de la Visitation

Location
Rue de la Visitation

To the N of the Basilique du Sacré-Cœur is the neo-Romanesque Chapelle de la Visitation, its interior decorated with frescoes and mosaics. On this spot Marguerite-Marie is believed to have seen her first visions.
In the side chapel on the right can be seen the glass sarcophagus containing the saint's remains.

Musée du Hiéron

Location
Rue de la Paix

Opening times
15 Apr.–15 Oct.,
9 a.m.–noon and 2–7 p.m.

Admission charge

A short distance N of the Chapelle de la Visitation is the Musée du Hiéron, a museum of religious art containing Italian, French and Flemish paintings of the 16th–18th c. and a notable 12th c. tympanum from the nearby abbey of Anzy-le-Duc (20 km (12½ miles) S; fine Romanesque church, in spite of damage caused during the Revolution).

Town Hall

Location
Place Guignaud

The Hôtel de Ville (Town Hall), in the centre of the town, is a magnificent Renaissance building of 1525, also known as the Maison Jayet after the family which originally built it. Particularly notable is the main front facing the square, built of yellowish stone, with rich figural decoration and numerous portrait medallions of French kings.

Tour St-Nicolas

On the N side of the square rises the Tour St-Nicolas (16th c.), with a slate-roofed steeple – a relic of a church which is now almost totally destroyed.

Digoin

Situation
12 km (7½ miles) W

The little industrial town of Digoin lies at the junction of the Bourbince with the Loire. This is an important junction on the French inland waterways system, at the meeting of the Canal du Centre, the 56 km (35 mile) long canal from Roanne to Digoin, and the rivers Loire, Bourbince and Arroux.
An interesting feature of the town is the Pont-Canal, the aqueduct carrying the Bourbince over the Loire. An attractive riverside path lined with robinias leads from the centre of the town to the aqueduct (built 1834–38), which spans the Loire

Aqueduct over the Loire, Digoin

with its 11 arches, covering a total length of 243 m (266 yd).
The canal is 6 m (20 ft) wide and 2 m (6½ ft) deep.
An important contribution to the economy of Digoin is made by
the ceramic industry, which produces both industrial and art
ceramics. There is a documentation centre illustrating the
production processes and incorporating a museum of ceramic
products.

Le Puy

Region: Auvergne
Département: Haute-Loire
Altitude: 630 m (2067 ft)
Population: 30,000

Le Puy, chief town of the département of Haute-Loire, lies on
the eastern border of Auvergne in the district of Velay, a region
shaped by volcanic activity. The little River Borne flows past
the old town to join the Loire a little way to the E. Le Puy is a
great lace-making centre.

Situation

Dominated by its Cathedral and the bizarre towering pinnacles
of the Rocher Corneille and the Aiguilhe St-Michel, two
weathered volcanic cones, the town presents a unique and
extraordinary aspect. A walk round the old town – illuminated
after dark – is an experience not to be missed.

** The town

Le Puy: general view

History

Le Puy, centre of the episcopal diocese of Velay, was founded in the 6th c., and has been a noted pilgrimage centre since the 10th c. with its Black Virgin (pilgrimage on 15 August). The town also lay on the pilgrims' route to Santiago de Compostela in north-western Spain, and the chapel of St Michael on its high rock pinnacle was founded by the bishop of Le Puy in 962 after he himself had made the pilgrimage to Santiago.

* Cathedral

The famous Cathédrale Notre-Dame, pilgrimage centre and episcopal see, stands on higher ground above the old town, at the foot of the Rocher Corneille. Built at the end of the 12th c., it shows a mingling of Auvergnat Romanesque and the architecture of south-western France, with clear Byzantine influence.

Exterior

A broad flight of steps, relaid in the 19th c., ascends past the old Hôtel-Dieu (Hospice) on the left to the W front of the Cathedral, of coloured volcanic stone, with a porch leading through three arches into the nave and aisles. The doorways into the aisles have beautiful carved 12th c. doors. The steps continue up the centre of the porch, in the vaulting of which are 13th c. paintings, showing Byzantine influence, of the Virgin and Child (left) and the Transfiguration (right).

The steps come to an end in front of the former principal doorway of the Cathedral, which was walled up in 1780. From here a flight of steps on the right leads up to the present entrance in the S aisle.

The dark colour of the stone, the sparse lighting and the massive proportions of the structure give the interior of the Cathedral a dim and mysterious aspect. An effect of great solemnity is produced by the succession of heavy ribbed arches and tall domes lit only by small windows. The works of art in the side chapels are almost totally invisible in the darkness.

On the W wall, above the original entrance is a gilded Baroque relief of St Andrew. Farther along, in the aisles, are two large Baroque pictures: on the left a picture by Jean Solvain painted after an outbreak of plague in 1629, on the right a similar picture painted by Jean François in 1653 after another outbreak.

A doorway in the N aisle leads into the Chapelle des Reliques (at present in course of restoration), which has a 15th c. wall painting depicting the Seven Liberal Arts (grammar, rhetoric and dialectic; arithmetic, geometry, music and astronomy).

At the crossing (dome rebuilt) is the Baroque high altar (1723), with a figure of the Virgin which has replaced the original Black Virgin (burned during the French Revolution) as an object of pilgrimage.

The Porche du For, in the E wall of the S transept, leads into the little Place du For, a square high above the town and from which there is a superb view.

At the E end of the S aisle is the Sacristy, which houses the Cathedral treasury, poorer than it was as a result of the

Interior

Place du For

Treasury

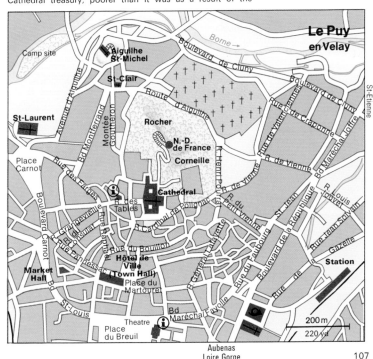

Aubenas
Loire Gorge

Revolution. Its greatest treasure is the celebrated Bible of Théodulf, a magnificent example of Carolingian book illumination. The manuscript was written in the 8th c., probably at St Benoît-sur-Loire (see entry) – then the abbey of Fleury – and takes its name from St Théodulf, bishop of Orléans and abbot of Fleury, one of the leading figures of the Carolingian Renaissance. Another important item is a copy of the Black Virgin which was destroyed in 1789; although the faces are blackened by the smoke of votive candles, the hands, protected by the numerous garments in which the Virgin was clothed, have preserved their original colouring. The Sacristy also contains liturgical objects, pictures and sculpture.

Porche St-Jean

From the N transept the Porche St-Jean, with parchment-covered and iron-studded doors, leads out of the Cathedral. Opposite the doorway is the Baptistère St-Jean (11th–12th c.), in front of the entrance to which are two stone lions. In the adjoining Maison du Prieur (Prior's Lodging) is a small folk museum. Turning left from here, we enter the cloister.

Cloister

The Cloister, built against the N side of the Cathedral, with richly carved capitals, shows a variety of stylistic influences, including Byzantine elements. It achieves an impressive effect by the use of different colours of stone.

In the Chapelle des Morts, on the E side of the cloister, is a large wall painting of the Crucifixion (13th c.). The E side has an ornamental wrought-iron grille of the Romanesque period. Good view of the statue of the Virgin on top of the Rocher Corneille.

View of Cathedral from Rocher Corneille

In the former Salle des Etats (Hall of the States), over the cloister, is the Trésor d'Art Religieux (Treasury of Religious Art). Among notable items in the collection are a genealogy of Christ painted on parchment and two sumptuous garments for the Black Virgin, one being 15th c. Oriental work with a representation of the Tree of Jesse, the other local work of the 18th c. with rich gold and silver brocade ornament.

*Rocher Corneille

From the N transept of the Cathedral it is only a few paces to the gate at the foot of the steep ascent (c. 15 minutes) to the top of the Rocher Corneille, a volcanic cone rising above the Cathedral to a height of 757 m (2484 ft) which has been left isolated by the erosion of the softer rock surrounding it.

Opening times
1 May–30 Sept., daily
9 a.m.–7 p.m.
1 Oct.–30 Apr., daily
9 a.m.–6 p.m.

Admission charge

From the summit plateau there are magnificent panoramic views (telescopes, orientation table, tape-recorded "guide parlant"). On the top, in lat. 45°2'54" N and long. 1°32'55" E, stands a red statue of the Virgin (Notre-Dame de France), a landmark visible far and wide. The figure, of cast iron, was erected in 1860; it is 16 m (52 ft) high (with base 22.70 m – 74 ft) and weighs some 110 tonnes. A narrow spiral staircase runs up inside the statue.

Notre-Dame de France

**Aiguilhe St-Michel

To the N of the Cathedral, near the River Borne, is another relic of former volcanic activity, the slender basaltic pinnacle of the Aiguilhe St-Michel. At its foot stands the Chapelle St-Clair (12th c.).
A steep stepped path hewn from the rock leads up in some 15 minutes to the Chapelle St-Michel (originally 10th c.), daringly sited on the highest point of the crag. The tower and the richly decorated façade of coloured volcanic stone were added in the 12th c. The interior has an irregular layout, adjusted to the cramped conditions on the summit. There are excellently preserved frescoes in the ambulatory, above the entrance and in the rectangular chancel. From the path which encircles the chapel there are fine views, particularly of the Rocher Corneille.

Opening times
16 Mar.–14 June, daily
10 a.m.–noon and 2–6 p.m.;
15 June–15 Sept., daily
9 a.m.–noon and 2–7 p.m.;
16 Sept.–2 Nov., daily
10 a.m.–noon and 2–6 p.m.

Admission charge

Church of St-Laurent

To the S of the Aiguilhe St-Michel, on the NW side of the old town, is the Gothic church of St-Laurent, originally a Dominican foundation. In the choir is the tomb of Bertrand Du Guesclin (c. 1320–1380), who drove the English out of most of their French possessions between 1370 and 1373.

Location
Place St-Laurent

Opening times
Temporarily closed

Lace Museum

Near the church of St-Laurent, to the E of the Place St-Laurent, is the Atelier-Conservatoire National de la Dentelle à la Main, where visitors can watch lace-makers at work and can see a collection of lace from the 17th c. to the present day.

Location
2 rue Du Guesclin

Chapelle St-Michel l'Aiguilhe

Detail of façade

Opening times
daily except Sat. and Sun.

In the same building are the Ecole Municipale de Musique (Municipal School of Music) and Ecole Municipale des Beaux-Arts (Municipal School of Fine Art).

Musée Crozatier

Location
Rue Antoine-Martin

Opening times
1 May–30 Sept., Wed.–Mon.
10 a.m.–noon and 2–6 p.m.;
1 Oct.–31 Jan. and
1 Mar.–30 Apr., Wed.–Mon
10 a.m.–noon and 2–4 p.m.

Admission charge

Some distance to the S of the town centre, at the far end of the large Jardin Henri Vinay which extends beyond the spacious Place du Breuil, is the Musée Crozatier, with a large and varied collection which includes numerous fossils, Romanesque and Gothic sculpture, faience and enamels, and an excellent collection of hand-made lace. The department of fine art has numbers of pictures of the 14th–18th c.

Near the museum, in the gardens, is a Romanesque doorway from Vorey priory.

Roanne

Region: Rhône-Alpes
Département: Loire
Altitude: 280 m (919 ft)
Population: 57,000

Situation

The industrial town of Roanne (textiles, papermaking, ceramics, mechanical engineering, arms manufacture) lies in an extensive plain on the left bank of the upper Loire, some 80 km (50 miles) N of St-Etienne. The Canal de Roanne à Digoin is an important inland waterway which runs parallel to the W bank of the Loire for 56 km (35 miles), with a port at Roanne. Around the town is a prosperous cattle-farming region.

Musée Joseph Déchelette

This museum, in the centre of the town, is named after the Roanne-born archaeologist Joseph Déchelette (1862–1914), who bequeathed his collections to the town.
The exhibits include prehistoric and Gallo-Roman material, medieval painting and sculpture, Roanne faience, Egyptian antiquities and a natural history collection. The museum has a specialist archaeological library.

Location
Rue Anatole-France

Opening times
Wed.–Mon. 10 a.m.–noon and 2–6 p.m.

Admission charge

Place Clemenceau

The Place Clemenceau is the central feature of the old town of Roanne. On the N side of the square is a keep, partly preserved, which formed part of the town's 11th c. fortifications. Opposite it, to the S, stands the 19th c. church of St-Etienne, beyond which is a pedestrian zone.

Charlieu

The ancient little town of Charlieu, on the right bank of the Sornin, has notable remains of a Benedictine abbey – the church (11th–12th c.), with a richly decorated porch, and the charming cloister.
In the western outskirts of the town there is another notable cloister belonging to a former Franciscan friary (14th–15th c.).

Situation
20 km (12½ miles) NE

St-Benoît-sur-Loire

Region: Centre
Département: Loiret
Altitude: 100 m (328 ft)
Population: 2000

The village of St-Benoît lies off the main road on the right bank of the Loire, some 30 km (19 miles) E of Orléans. it is noted for its large Benedictine abbey.

Situation

The abbey was a very ancient foundation, its origins going back to the 7th c. In the early medieval period the versatile and greatly gifted Théodulf (c. 750–821), a native of Catalonia, was bishop of Orléans and abbot of St-Benoît (then known as Fleury), and one of the leading figures of the Carolingian Renaissance.

History

** Abbey church

The large Romanesque abbey church was built between 1026 and 1218. The modern buildings (1958, 1969) on the S side of the church are occupied by the monks who re-established this

Monastic buildings not open to public

111

St-Benoît

Figured capital, St-Benoît

Church, Germigny-des-Prés

Benedictine house after the last war (a priory from 1946, an abbey from 1959).

Exterior

The imposing porch consists of three aisles of equal height, each of three bays, and is surmounted by the massive tower with a pitched roof topped by the bell-cote. The interior of the porch is notable for the fine capitals of its cluster columns, with foliage or figural decoration.

Since the church is enclosed by monastic buildings the rest of the exterior cannot be seen by visitors.

Interior

The interior, surprisingly light, is of powerful effect in its severity and clarity. The nave and the tall, narrow aisles have ribbed vaulting, reflecting the transition from Romanesque to Gothic, as far as the transept. The organ gallery was a later addition.

Beyond the transept is the long Romanesque choir, surrounded by an ambulatory with round-headed vaulting. A notable feature is the pavement of polychrome stone. On the left is the marble tomb of Philippe II (1052–1108), with a recumbent figure of the king supported by lions.

Crypt

The dark crypt (11th c.), its vaulting borne on squat and massive piers, reflects the ground plan of the apse. In the centre is a metal shrine (modern) containing the relics of St Benedict, brought here from the Italian abbey of Monte Cassino in the late 7th c.

Châteauneuf-sur-Loire

The little town of Châteauneuf-sur-Loire (reached from St-Benoît by way of Germigny-des-Prés, see below) huddles round the remains of a château (rebuilt in the 18th c.), set in a park containing a magnificent collection of rhododendrons. The old Salle des Gardes (Guard Room) now houses a museum (Musée de la Marine de Loire) devoted to shipping on the Loire.

In the parish church (12th–13th c.) is the marble tomb of the Marquis de la Vrillière (1672–1725), minister of Louis XIV.

Situation
10 km (6 miles) NW

Germigny-des-Prés

The village of Germigny-des-Prés lies between St-Benoît and Châteauneuf-sur-Loire. Near the main road is a church which is claimed to be the oldest in France – dating originally from Carolingian times but later rebuilt. In the dome of the choir chapel is a fine mosaic which is ascribed to the 9th c. Ravenna school.

Situation
5 km (3 miles) NW

St-Etienne

Region: Rhône-Alpes
Département: Loire
Altitude: 520 m (1706 ft)
Population: 220,000

St-Etienne, chief town of the département of Loire, lies on the little River Furan just to the E of the upper Loire, some 60 km (37 miles) SW of Lyons. A university town as well as a busy industrial city (metallurgy, motor vehicle construction, glassworks), it is the principal centre in the Loire coalfield.

Situation

Musée d'Art et d'Industrie

The Musée d'Art et d'Industrie (Museum of Art and Industry), to the S of the city centre, has four departments, each concerned with a field of importance to St-Etienne – coalmining (with a reproduction of coal-workings in the basement), arms technology, textile production and two-wheeled vehicles.

The museum also contains a collection of modern art (Impressionists, Cubists, Fauves, abstract paintings) and old masters.

Location
Place Louis-Comte

Opening times
Wed.–Mon. 10 a.m.–noon and 2–5 p.m.

Admission charge

Grangent

A short distance from St-Etienne is one of the few dams on the Loire: the Barrage de Grangent, which forms the long straggling Lac de Grangent, most of it enclosed by forest. On a hill which is now an island in the lake are the ruins of the 12th c. Château de Grangent.

Situation
10 km (6 miles) W

Lac de Grangent

Montbrison

Situation
36 km (22 miles) NW

The ancient little town of Montbrison is built round a hill on the border between the Loire plain and the Forez hills. In the S of the town, near the little River Vizézy which traverses it, is the church of Notre-Dame d'Espérance, an early 13th c. Gothic structure with a Flamboyant (Late Gothic) doorway added in the 15th c.

In the beautifully proportioned interior are the tombs of Pierre de Vernet and Guy IV.

Beyond the apse is the "Diana", originally the chapterhouse but now occupied by a library, which was built on the occasion of the marriage of Count Jean I (1296). The magnificent vaulted timber roof with its painted panels was installed in 1728.

To the W, on the boulevard which encircles the town, is the Musée d'Allard, with a fine collection of puppets and marionettes and a mineral cabinet. Beyond the museum extends the Parc d'Allard.

Montrond-les-Bains

Situation
22 km (14 miles) N

The little health resort of Montrond-les-Bains lies on the right bank of the Loire below the ruins of a 14th–16th c. castle. From here there are good views of the Forez hills and the Parc Régional du Pilat.

Parc Régional du Pilat

This nature park (area 65,000 hectares – 160,000 acres), named after the Mont Pilat massif in the centre of the area, was established in 1974. The Mont Pilat range separates the Loire from the Rhône to the E, reaching heights of 1370 m (4495 ft) in the Crêt de l'Oeillon to the NE and 1432 m (4698 ft) in the Crêt de la Perdrix. On the northern flank of the mountains are a number of artificial lakes formed by dams.

Situation
c. 5–30 km (3–20 miles) SE

St-Galmier

The little town of St-Galmier, with mineral springs which yield a well-known table water, lies on the River Coise, a few kilometres E of the *route nationale* from St-Etienne to Roanne. It has a notable church in Flamboyant style (15th–17th c.), with a beauiful Virgin of the Pillar and a Flemish triptych.

Situation
16 km (10 miles) N

St-Nazaire

Region: Pays de la Loire
Département: Loire-Atlantique
Altitude: sea level
Population: 70,000

The important industrial town and port of St-Nazaire lies at the mouth of the Loire. To the N extends the Grande Brière nature reserve, a large expanse of mainly marshy country.

Situation

With the great expansion of industry in the 19th c. St-Nazaire developed from a small fishing village into a considerable shipbuilding centre. Since even the lower reaches of the Loire were too shallow for the large vessels then being built, the harbour of St-Nazaire was substantially enlarged and developed; it now serves as the outer harbour for Nantes. During the Second World War the occupying German forces established a large submarine base here, and in the later years of the war St-Nazaire was totally destroyed. After the war it was rebuilt on a new and spacious plan.

History

Port

The busy port of St-Nazaire has a series of docks on the right bank of the Loire. A good general view of the port and the former submarine base can be had from the viewing platform between the Bassin de St-Nazaire and the river.
Near the Avant-Port (Outer Harbour) is a large expanse of beach.

*Loire Bridge

At the point where the Loire flows into the Atlantic the estuary is spanned by a road bridge constructed in 1972–75. With a total length of 2636 m (2883 yd) and a height of up to 61 m

Location
E of port installations

Loire Bridge, St-Nazaire

Toll

(200 ft), it is a notable example of modern civil engineering. From the bridge there are fine views on either side.

Grande Brière (Nature Reserve)

Extent
Some 20 km (12½ miles) N

The Grande Brière was once an inlet of the sea, scattered with numerous islands. It is now a great expanse of marsh, bog and moorland, partly drained by a network of canals, with a distinctive flora and fauna (many water birds).
The Parc Régional Naturel Brière, a nature reserve with an area of 40,000 hectares (100,000 acres), was established in 1970.

Pornic

Location
30 km (19 miles) S

The Loire Bridge (see above) leads from St-Nazaire to St-Brevin-les-Pins, from which the road continues parallel to the coast (numerous beaches), some distance inland.
Pornic, on the Côte de Jade (Jade Coast), is a popular holiday resort on the Baie de Bourgneuf, into which flows the Canal de Haute Perche. On the E side of the town is the fishing harbour, and on the W, near the beach, the Château, once surrounded by a moat. Outside the town to the W are the prehistoric "Druids' Stones".
From Pornic there are boat services to the island of Noirmoutier (see entry).

Sancerre and its vineyards

Sancerre

Region: Centre
Département: Cher
Altitude: 310 m (1017 ft)
Population: 2500

The little old-world town of Sancerre, some 50 km (30 miles) NE of Bourges, is beautifully situated on the last hill of an upland region covered with vineyards, looking out over the wide Loire plain. The dry white wine produced here goes well with fish and seafood. Some of the *caves* in which the wine is made can be visited, and also the dairies which produce goat's-milk cheese. Many artists and craftsmen have settled in the old houses in the town.

Situation

The town

Sancerre, a small town of narrow streets, is best seen on foot. Cars can be parked below the town walls, half-way up the hill. The recommended route is marked by green arrows.

The Beffroi (Belfry) which stands in the centre of the town is an old keep built in 1509, now the bell-tower of the neo-Romanesque church of Notre-Dame.

Beffroi

Saumur

Tour des Fiefs

On the E side of the town, in the park of the château, is the Tour des Fiefs, a prominent landmark visible from a considerable distance. Commanding extensive views, it is the last remnant of a 14th c. castle; it is privately owned, and is open to the public only on Sundays and public holidays from 2 p.m. onwards.

Esplanade Porte César

On the NE side of Sancerre, adjoining the park of the château, is the Esplanade Porte César, a small tree-shaded square from which there is a panoramic view of the Loire valley. To the left is the beginning of the road which runs round the old walls.

Saumur

Region: Pays de la Loire
Département: Maine-et-Loire
Altitude: 30 m (98 ft)
Population: 25,000

Situation

Picturesquely situated on the left bank of the Loire and an island in the river, some 50 km (30 miles) E of Angers, Saumur is a commercial town, dealing mainly in the wine, both still and sparkling, produced in the surrounding area. The *caves* in which the wine is made can be visited. Saumur, where a cavalry school was first established in 1763, is also known as the home of the famous cavalry unit, the "Cadre Noir". Much of its achitecture is in French classical style.

Place de la République

The Place de la République, by the river, is bounded on the SW by the two buildings constituting the Hôtel de Ville (Town Hall). The one on the left, which dates from the 16th c., has a rather fortress-like aspect with its blank walls, few windows and corner towers. On the right-hand side of the square is the classical-style theatre. From the Pont Cessart, which leads to the Ile d'Offard, an island now densely packed with houses, there is a very fine view of the old town, and the château rearing up behind it.

Church of St-Pierre

Location
Place St-Pierre

The church of St-Pierre stands in the old town, a little way SE of the Town Hall. Originally Romanesque, it was partly rebuilt in the 17th c. It contains 16th c. tapestries.

*Château

Location
Above the old town

Opening times
Daily 9–11.30 a.m. and 2–6 p.m.; also at Easter and Whitsun from 8.30 p.m.

Admission charge

The road up to the château, standing high above the town, is marked by green lines on the roadway. There is also a footpath (signposted) from the old town.

The Château de Saumur, with three wings laid out round a courtyard open to the NW, flanked by four corner towers and defended by massive bastions, rises above the old town to the SE. It was built in the 14th c. on the site of a 12th c. castle belonging to Geoffrey Plantagenet. The French king Jean le

Château and church of St-Pierre, Saumur

Bon had granted his son Louis the duchy of Anjou, and Louis resolved to build in Saumur a château which should equal in splendour the châteaux of his brothers.

Of the original 12th c. castle, designed purely for military purposes, the 14th c. rebuilding preserved only the outer walls, enclosing an irregular polygon, and the basement storey.
On the side facing the hill the château is cut off from the neighbouring country by a deep ditch. From the NW corner of the carefully maintained outer ward there is a fine view of the town and the river. On the side facing the valley are massive retaining walls.
The courtyard of the château is reached by way of a large entrance gateway and a short vaulted passage. Diagonally across from the entrance is the famous Late Gothic tower housing a spiral staircase (note the interesting terminal boss of the vaulting). To the left of the tower is a small well-house, with wooden winding gear. On the right-hand side of the courtyard are the entrances to the cellars lying under the courtyard and to the Tour du Guet.

Exterior

The Tour du Guet (Watch-Tower) which rises above the SW wing of the château can be climbed on a succession of spiral staircases and passages. From the platform there are views down into the courtyard of the château and over the roofs of the town and the valley beyond.

Tour du Guet

The château houses two museums. On the first floor is the Musée des Arts Décoratifs (Museum of Decorative Art), with sculpture, tapestries, enamels and ceramics of the medieval and

Museums

119

Renaissance periods. On the second floor is the Musée International du Cheval (International Museum of the Horse), with a wide variety of exhibits related to horses and riding, including particularly saddles, harness, uniforms, etc.

Church of Notre-Dame de Nantilly

Location
Rue de Nantilly

The church of Notre-Dame de Nantilly stands on the S side of the town, to the W of the Jardin des Plantes (Botanic Garden). This Romanesque church (12th c.), with Gothic alterations, contains fine tapestries of the 15th–17th c. and a 12th c. wooden figure of the Virgin.

Chênehutte-les-Tuffeaux

Situation
8 km (5 miles) NW

Chênehutte-les-Tuffeaux, on the left bank of the Loire, has a notable Romanesque church. Visitors can also see round the interesting mushroom farms, housed in underground quarries. There is a small museum of mushroom culture.

*Cunault

Situation
13 km (8 miles) NW

The abbey church (11th–13th c.) of Cunault is a superb example of Romanesque architecture. The Benedictine house to which it belonged was dissolved in the 18th c. The interior is notable for the clarity of its forms and the richly carved capitals of its tall columns (binoculars required for a good view). There are remains of Romanesque and Gothic frescoes in the apsidal domes. On the S side of the ambulatory is a 13th c. reliquary of painted wood.

In the surrounding area there are many man-made caves and shafts in the rock, used as wine-cellars or for mushroom growing; some of them are open to visitors.

Dénezé-sous-Doué

Situation
18 km (11 miles) W

The village of Dénezé-sous-Doué – best reached from Saumur by way of Doué-la-Fontaine – is noted for its Caverne Sculptée (open 2.30–6 p.m., in summer to 8 p.m.; admission charge), with numerous relief carvings by unknown 16th c. craftsmen. There are numbers of cave dwellings in the area.

Montreuil-Bellay

Situation
16 km (10 miles) S

The little town of Montreuil-Bellay, still partly surrounded by walls, lies on the River Thouet, a left-bank tributary of the Loire. Near the river is the old castle, once enclosed within a ring of walls and round towers. The right-hand gateway leads to the Late Gothic chapel, the one on the left to the main castle buildings (13th–15th c.). A good general view of the castle precincts can be had from the bridge over the Thouet, to the N.

Château de Saumur

Moulin de la Herpinière

Prime Meridian

At the village of Souzay-Champigny the road crosses the Prime Meridian (sign), the line of zero longitude (0°) running through Greenwich Observatory, near London; this was internationally recognised in 1911 as the starting-point for the measurement of longitude.

Here, too, the steep rock faces have been gouged out to make wine cellars and troglodytic dwellings (photograph, p. 29). A few kilometres S of the road skirting the river is the Moulin de la Herpinière (signpost), a restored windmill now housing a collection of old tools and implements and an artist's studio.

Location
6 km (4¼ miles) E

Sully-sur-Loire

Region: Centre
Département: Loiret
Altitude: 120 m (394 ft)
Population: 6000

The busy little town of Sully lies on the left bank of the Loire approximately half-way between Gien and Orléans, at the position of an old ford.

Situation

In the year 1429 Charles VII, nominally king of France since 1422, though the title had been usurped by Henry V of England in 1420, was staying in Sully, and it was here that Jeanne d'Arc, after defeating the English at Patay on 18 June,

History

finally persuaded him to have himself crowned as king. The coronation took place at Reims on 17 July.

In the 18th c. Sully several times provided a refuge for the young Voltaire, who had made himself unpopular with the court in Paris by his biting epigrams.

Château

Location
Chemin de la Salle-Verte

Opening times
1–31 Mar., daily
10–11.45 a.m. and 2–5 p.m.;
1 Apr.–30 Sept., daily
9–11.45 a.m. and 2–6 p.m.;
1–31 Oct., daily
9–11.45 a.m. and 2–4.30 p.m.

Conducted tours

Admission charge

Interior

The Château de Sully, surrounded by a moat, was originally built in the 14th c. In 1602 it was acquired by Maximilien de Béthune (from 1606 Duc de Sully), who had fought in the Huguenot armies from 1576 onwards and as a minister under Henri IV had brought order into the national finances. In spite of the extensions which he carried out the château shows remarkable unity of style.

An imposing structure situated directly on the river and flanked by round towers with pointed conical roofs, the château is surrounded by a moat, which merges on the E side into a picturesque elongated lake. Outside the entrance front is a lawn, with a statue of the Duc de Sully. SE from this is an ornamental bastion from which there is an attractive view.

The main gateway leads into the courtyard, with the wings of the château on three sides and a low wall on the far side.

In the entrance wing, to the left, is the Grand Salon, with a painted coffered ceiling, and above this, on the first floor, is another saloon with a large chimneypiece and also a painted coffered ceiling, in which the figure of Zeus in the form of an eagle hurling thunderbolts frequently recurs.

Château de Sully from the SE

The right-hand wing is entered from the courtyard. To the left of the doorway, which is flanked by semicircular towers, is a tablet commemorating Jeanne d'Arc's stay here on 21–22 June 1429. Then comes the Salle des Gardes (Guard Room). Above this, on the first floor, is the Salle d'Honneur (Grand Hall), with portraits of Sully's Béthune ancestors. Adjoining is the small domestic chapel, containing the double tomb (reproduction), in marble, of Sully and his wife. Also on this floor is the Duke's bedroom, decorated in blue, with two tapestries and (over the chimneypiece) an equestrian portrait of Henri IV. Of particular interest is the magnificent timber roof (1363), constructed of chestnut, a wood immune to damage by pests. Along the N side of the top storey runs a narrow sentry-walk.

From the NW corner of the moat a suspension bridge crosses the river; (this bridge collapsed in 1985 but is being rebuilt). From the far side there is a fine panoramic view.

Bridge over the Loire

Tours

Region: Centre
Département: Indre-et-Loire
Altitude: 50 m (164 ft)
Population: 145,000

Tours, capital of the old province of Touraine, the "garden of France", a university town and the see of an archbishop, chief town of the département of Indre-et-Loire, lies astride both these rivers just to the E of their junction, approximately half-way between Orléans and Angers.

Situation

In Roman times Tours was known as Caesarodunum and later as Urbs Turonum (after the local Gallic people, the Turones). In the 3rd c. Christianity was brought to the town by St Gatianus (Gatien), and in the 4th c. the preaching of St Martin made it a great ecclesiastical centre. Around the church containing St Martin's tomb there grew up the town of Martinopolis (later known as Châteauneuf), which then amalgamated with the Roman settlement to form the town of Tours. In 732, in the battle of Tours and Poitiers, the Moors who had advanced over the Pyrenees into France were defeated by Charles Martel. During the Carolingian Renaissance there was a celebrated school of painting in Tours.
In medieval times the town was temporarily held by the English, but in 1243 it was recovered by France, and from then until the 16th century almost all the French kings resided from time to time in Tours.

History

*Cathedral

The Cathédrale St-Gatien, which stands to the E of the old town centre, is dedicated to the first bishop of Tours. Begun in the 12th c., it was not completed until the 16th.

Location
Place de la Cathédrale

The W front, flanked by two towers, has a central and two lateral doorways. The façade, in Flamboyant style, is overloaded with ornament; the towers with their lantern roofs already point towards the Renaissance. To the left is the Cloître de la Psalette

Exterior

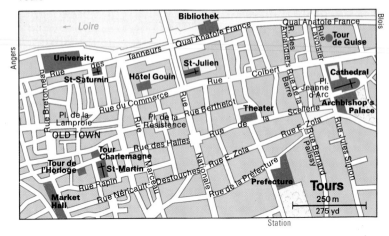

(15th–16th c.), which can normally be seen on application to the verger but is at present closed for restoration. Note the fine decorated buttresses, particularly in the choir.

Interior

The walls of the nave which rise above the aisles are almost completely occupied by windows. The choir and the chapels opening off the ambulatory have magnificent 13th c. stained glass. The rose windows in the N and S transepts are 14th c. In the ambulatory, adjoining the S transept, is the beautiful Renaissance marble tomb of two sons of Charles VII.

Archbishop's Palace

Location
Place de la Cathédrale

Opening times
Daily 9 a.m.–noon and
2–6 p.m. (Museum)

Admission charge

The old Archevêché (Archbishop's Palace) on the S side of the Cathedral dates in its present form from the 17th and 18th c. but incorporates some earlier work. It now houses the Musée des Beaux-Arts (Museum of Fine Art), with furniture, pictures and sculpture from Tours and its vicinity. Particularly notable are the Dutch and Italian paintings (Rembrandt, Mantegna).

*Old town

The older part of the town, Vieux Tours, lies to the W of the Rue Nationale, the town's main traffic artery, and to the S of the university quarter. The central feature of this quarter, which has been carefully restored with great attention to detail, is the Place Plumereau. A walk round the narrow streets between Rue Bretonneau and Rue Constantine will reveal numerous picturesque nooks and corners.

Tour de l'Horloge
Tour Charlemagne

The old church of St-Martin stood in the old town on a site now traversed by the Rue des Halles. The Tour de l'Horloge (Clock Tower) on the S side of the street and the Tour Charlemagne to

Stained glass in Tours Cathedral ▶

Place Plumereau

A shop in the old town

the NE are all that remains of the large 11th–13th c. church which fell into decay after the Wars of Religion. The new church, with the tomb of St Martin, is a neo-Romanesque/Byzantine structure of the late 19th c.

*Hôtel Gouin

One of the finest houses in the old town is the Hôtel Gouin, a little way E of the intersection of Rue Constantine and Rue du Commerce. This mansion of about 1510, largely based on Italian models, now houses the archaeological collection of the Société Archéologique de Touraine (open daily 9 a.m.–noon and 2–7 p.m.; admission charge).

Luynes

Situation
13 km (8 miles) W

The little town of Luynes, lying just off the N bank of the Loire, has a large château of the 15th and 16th c. (not open to the public). 1.5 km (1 mile) NE of the town are the ruins of a Roman aqueduct, a relic of the days when Luynes was a Roman fort. Some 10 km (6 miles) farther W, at Cinq-Mars-la-Pile, is a 29 m (95 ft) high tower which is probably also of Roman origin. On the road from Luynes to Cinq-Mars-la-Pile are numbers of dwellings and cellars hewn from the rock.

Vouvray

Situation
10 km (6 miles) E

The village of Vouvray, renowned for its wine, lies on the right bank of the Loire, surrounded by vineyards which produce only white wine. As at many places along the river, the wine-cellars are in tunnels driven horizontally into the soft local rock.

Ussé

Region: Centre
Département: Indre-et-Loire
Altitude: 45 m (148 ft)

The large château of Ussé stands in a secluded situation some 15 km (9 miles) N of Chinon on the Indre, here flowing parallel to the Loire, on the northern fringe of the extensive wooded area of the Forêt de Chinon.

Situation

*Château

When it was built in the 15th c. the Château d'Ussé formed a closed square; later, however, the N wing was pulled down and gave place to a terraced garden, from which there is a view over the little river and the wide valley beyond.
Ussé is believed to have been the model for the castle of the Sleeping Beauty in the fairy story by Charles Perrault (1628–1703), "La Belle au Bois Dormant".
There is a good view of the château from the bridge over the Indre.

The E side of the château still shows the fortess-like style of the late medieval period, but the wings to the W, added in the 16th c., have the lighter character of Renaissance architecture, more concerned with aesthetic effect than with functional needs.

Opening times
1 Mar.–30 Nov., daily 9 a.m.–noon and 2–7 p.m.;
1 Dec.–28 Feb., daily 9 a.m.–noon and 2–6 p.m.

Conducted tours

Admission charge

Exterior

Ussé, Castle of the Sleeping Beauty

The roof is richly patterned with its numerous pointed towers, chimneys and dormer windows.

Interior

The château, which is privately owned, is still inhabited. The rooms open to the public (notable among them the Chambre du Roi, the King's Bedroom) contain Beauvais, Aubusson and Flemish tapestries, old European and Oriental weapons, period furniture and pictures.

Chapel

In front of the 16th c. chapel are two huge cedars, said to have been brought to Ussé in 1808 by the writer and statesman François-René de Châteaubriand.

In the upper part of the doorway, which already shows strong Renaissance influence, are figures of the twelve Apostles. Inside, on the left-hand wall, is a 19th c. monument in neo-Gothic style; on the right is a Madonna in coloured faience by Luca della Robbia (1400–82).

Valençay

Region: Centre
Département: Indre
Altitude: 140 m (459 ft)
Population: 3000

Situation

The little town of Valençay lies approximately half-way between Bourges and Tours, at the base of the wide bend of the Loire between Nevers and Tours. The little River Nahon flows through the town.

Château

Opening times
Palm Sunday–31 Oct., daily
9–11.30 a.m. and 2–6.30
p.m.

Conducted tours

Admission charge

Son et lumière
See Practical Information

The Renaissance château of Valençay, set in a large park, lies to the SW of the town centre. It was built in 1540 by Philibert Delorme, the royal architect, who was also responsible for the construction of the Château de Fontainebleau (SE of Paris). In 1805 the property was bought by Talleyrand, Napoleon's celebrated foreign minister.

The château as we see it today consists of two wings set at right angles to one another, terminated at the W and S ends by large round towers with domed tops. It is clear that the original plan of the château was on a much larger scale and was only partly carried out. The main wing, which is reached by way of a drawbridge, shows the influence of the Italian Renaissance; the side wing, which has only two storeys, is Baroque. The remains of a medieval castle are believed to lie under the terrace, which commands extensive views.

Interior

Only the side wing is open to the public. On the ground floor is a gallery with Talleyrand family portraits. The adjoining rooms contain a large collection of Empire furniture. Within the base of the Tour Neuve (New Tower) at the end of the wing is the Music Room, with a small collection of porcelain. A spiral staircase (at the foot of which is Talleyrand's wheel-chair) leads to the upper floor, on which many personal mementoes of Talleyrand are displayed. The Chambre du Roi (King's Bedroom) has grisaille (grey monochrome, in relief) paintings.

Entrance wing, Château de Valençay

Porte St-Georges, Vendôme

The gallery on the upper floor is 77 m (253 ft) long. On the staircase is a tapestry with an allegorical representation of the French possessions in the West Indies.

In the park surrounding the château can be seen peacocks, wildfowl and other animals, including red deer in the remoter parts.

Park

Within the park, to the W of the château, is an interesting Automobile Museum, with vintage Amilcars, Bugattis, Delages, Panhards, etc., as well as old bicycles and motorcycles.

Automobile Museum

Nouans-les-Fontaines

The village of Nouans-les-Fontaines, in the valley of the Indrois, has a 13th c. church with a fine "Descent from the Cross" of the school of Jean Fouquet (15th c.).

Situation
23 km (14 miles) W

St-Aignan

This old-world little town on the Cher is dominated by a large château of the 13th–16th c. (not open to the public). From the terrace there are beautiful views of the valley and the river.
The church of St-Aignan, to the E of the château, dates from the 11th and 12th c. It has Early Gothic vaulting borne on Romanesque piers with figured capitals. The Romanesque crypt has frescoes of the 12th–15th c.

Situation
21 km (13 miles) NW

Selles-sur-Cher

Situation
14 km (9 miles) N

Of the abbey which once stood at Selles-sur-Cher there remains only the church, built in the 12th and 15th c. and largely rebuilt in the 17th c. after suffering severe destruction by fire during the Wars of Religion. In the apse is a curious carved frieze, depicting the life of St Eusice or Eusitius, to whom the church is dedicated, in the upper portion, and New Testament scenes in the lower. The saint's tomb is in the crypt.

The château, surrounded by walls and a moat, dates from the 13th c. but was rebuilt in the reign of Henri IV.

Vendôme

Region: Centre
Département: Loir-et-Cher
Altitude: 85 m (279 ft)
Population: 20,000

Situation

Vendôme, the Roman Vindocinum, is picturesquely situated on the Loir, a right-bank tributary of the Loire which is here divided into a number of arms, some 30 km (20 miles) NW of Blois. From the 9th c. it was the chief town of a county and between 1515 and 1727 of a duchy.

Old town

The old town of Vendôme, the Quartier Ancien, lies on an island between two arms of the Loir. On the W side of the Place St-Martin, in the centre of the old town, is the Tour St-Martin, all that remains of a Renaissance church pulled down in 1857. In Rue du Change, which leaves the NE corner of the square, is the Chapelle du Lycée (1452), adjoining which on the W is the classical-style Lycée Ronsard, originally a college of the Oratorians, at which the 8-year-old Honoré de Balzac was a pupil. At the end of Rue St-Jacques, which branches off on the left, stands the Madeleine church (1474).

*Trinité church

On the E side of the old town, a little way SE of the Place St-Martin, is the Trinité church, with a richly decorated façade. Originally a monastic church, it was built in the 12th–15th c. The free-standing Romanesque tower (80 m (262 ft) high) in front of the doorway dates from the 12th c.

Notable features of the finely proportioned interior are the large windows (some of them with old stained glass) and the richly carved choir-stalls (15th–16th c.).

On the S side of the church are the remains of a cloister of the 14th–15th c. The old monastic buildings now house a small museum of medieval and Renaissance religious art and a collection of material on the history of the region.

Château

Location
Place du Château

The Château de Vendôme, situated on a hill surrounded by trees, is reached from the S side of the old town by way of a handsome gateway, the Porte St-Georges.

Of the original castle, founded in the 9th c., there remain a number of towers and extensive stretches of walls dating from the 13th–15th c. and now enclosing attractive gardens. There are fine views from the highest of the towers and also from the footpaths on the hill (known as the "Montagne").

Opening times
Wed.–Mon. 9 a.m.–noon and 2–6 p.m.

Admission charge

Areines

On the other side of the Loir is the village of Areines, with a small church containing well-preserved Romanesque frescoes, some of them still in process of being freed from 18th c. overpainting.

Situation
3 km (2 miles) E

Villandry

Region: Centre
Département: Indre-et-Loire
Altitude: 95 m (312 ft)
Population: 800

The village of Villandry lies on the left bank of the Cher just above its junction with the Loire, 20 km (12½ miles) W of Tours.

Situation

Château

The 16th c. Château de Villandry is principally famed for its terraced gardens, now restored to their original form.
The paved area in front of the Cour d'Honneur (Grand Courtyard) is surrounded by a rectangular system of moats. A bridge leads into the courtyard, round which are the two-storey wings of the château. The side wings are arcaded and have richly decorated dormer windows. At the outer corner of the château, facing the gardens, is the massive square Donjon (Keep), the oldest part of the structure (14th c.). Outside to the right, are the stables.

Opening times
Daily 8 a.m.–noon and 2–6 p.m.

Conducted tours

Admission charge

The state apartments have 18th c. furniture, tapestries and Italian and Spanish paintings of the Renaissance and Baroque periods.
A particularly notable feature is the Hispano-Mauresque ceiling of carved, painted and gilded cedar wood in the Grand

Interior

Villandry and its gardens

Villandry
Garden of Love

Tender love
(hearts, flames)

Wild love
(misshapen hearts)

Tragic love
(swords, daggers)

Fleeting love
(fans, letters)

The gardens of Villandry

Gallery. The ceiling originally came from a 13th c. Spanish mosque; in the 16th c. it was fitted into a Christian chapel, with the addition of the scallop shells of St James and the arms of the Spanish provinces which can still be seen; and finally, having been dismantled, the ceiling was acquired by the owner of Villandry and installed in its present position by a local craftsman – a task which took 15 years.

The gardens

From the upper floor of the château a stone staircase leads down to the highest part of the gardens, which have a total area of 5 hectares (12¼ acres). From here there is an excellent view of the whole layout: to the left the ornamental gardens, in the foreground the "Garden of Love" and beyond this, on a lower level on the far side of the moat, the vegetable gardens. These are very different from the normal kitchen garden. This is because in the 16th c. rare species of vegetables, mostly imported from abroad, were grown here; because of their rarity they were planted near the château, where a watch could be kept on them; but in order not to offend the aesthetic sense of the owners of the château the beds were laid out in the form of an ornamental garden. The vegetables are still grown in the same fashion, using no artificial fertilisers, and sold to visitors.

Savonnières

Situation
2 km (1¼ miles) E

At the near end of the village of Savonnières is the entrance to the Caves Gouttières (open daily 9 a.m.–noon and 2–6 p.m.; admission charge), two stalactitic caves with beautiful sinter formations.

Practical Information

Access

From the northern Channel ports via Paris, then A10 motorway
to Orléans and Tours, or N7 to Nevers.
From the E via Beaune and Autun to Nevers.
Suggested routes: see p. 28.

By car

Of the towns described in this Guide only St-Etienne and
Nantes are served by scheduled air services, flown by Air
France and the French domestic airline Air Inter. There are
direct flights from London to Nantes (Air France), domestic
flights to Nantes from Paris, Avignon, Lyons, Marseilles, Nice
and Strasbourg, and domestic flights to St-Etienne only from
Paris.

By air

The best approach is via Paris, from which there are services via
Gien, Nevers and Moulins to Le Puy and via Orléans, Tours and
Nantes to St-Nazaire.
Since many of the places of interest are not on the main lines,
however, rail travel is not to be recommended as a means of
seeing the sights of the Loire valley.

By rail

Airlines

International routes are flown by the French national airline, Air
France; domestic routes by Air Inter. Both companies have
desks at all French commercial airports; outside France
information about Air Inter services can be obtained from Air
France offices.

Head office:
1 Square Max-Hymans,
F-75741 Paris Cedex 15;
tel. (1) 2 73 41 41

Air France

Great Britain:
158 New Bond Street,
London W1Y 0AY;
tel. (01) 499 8611 and 499 9511

United States:
666 Fifth Avenue,
New York, NY 10019;
tel. (212) 841 7301

Canada:
Montreal Trust Building, Suite 704,
100 Sparks Street,
Ottawa;
tel. (613) 236 0689 and 236 0601

Paris:
91 Avenue des Champs-Elysées;
tel. (1) 7 78 14 14

British Airways

Bicycle hire

Since the châteaux which are the most visited attractions in the Loire valley almost all lie within a relatively small area they can readily be seen on a cycle tour.

Bicycles can be hired from private firms in many towns and also at railway stations (see Rail services).

Package arrangements covering the hire of a bicycle and overnight accommodation are also available: information can be obtained from tourist offices (see Information).

Camping

Camping is a more popular form of holiday in France than in other European countries. Practically every place of any tourist interest has at least one camp site (*terrain de camping*), and frequently several. Sites are classified with one to four stars according to the facilities and amenities they offer. During the main holiday season sites on the most popular routes are usually full (*complet*), but it will almost always be possible to find room on a site somewhere in the surrounding countryside, a little off the beaten track.

Since camp sites are so numerous it is not possible, nor necessary, to list them here.

Car hire

Avis

13 rue Max-Richard,
F-49000 Angers;
tel. (41) 88 20 24

6 rue Jean-Moulin,
F-41000 Blois;
tel. (54) 74 48 15

23 Avenue Henri-Laudier,
F-18000 Bourges;
tel. (48) 24 38 84

18 Boulevard de Stalingrad,
F-44000 Nantes;
tel. (40) 74 07 65

Aéroport de Nantes
tel. (40) 75 84 60

5 rue de la Passière,
F-58000 Nevers;
tel. (86) 57 51 03

13 rue des Sansonnières,
F-45000 Orléans;
tel. (38) 62 27 04

16 Boulevard Jules-Ferry,
F-42300 Roanne;
tel. (77) 71 84 95

27 Avenue Denfert-Rochereau,
F-42000 St-Etienne;
tel. (77) 32 09 61

Aéroport de St-Etienne
tel. (77) 32 09 61

126 Avenue de la République,
F-44600 St-Nazaire;
tel. (40) 66 65 44

39 bis Boulevard Heurteloup,
F-37000 Tours;
tel. (47) 05 59 33

26 Boulevard du Général-de-Gaulle,   EuropCar
F-49000 Angers;
tel. (41) 88 80 80

29 Avenue Jean-Jaurès,
F-18000 Bourges;
tel. (48) 24 02 94

18 rue de Lyon,
F-03000 Moulins;
tel. (70) 44 30 12

6 Allée des Tanneurs,
F-44000 Nantes;
tel. (40) 48 45 23

Aéroport de Nantes
tel. (40) 75 01 97

49 Faubourg de Paris,
F-58000 Nevers;
tel. (86) 59 02 32

Les Trois Fontaines,
F-45000 Orléans;
tel. (38) 88 08 08

3 Avenue de la Dentelle,
F-43000 Le Puy;
tel. (71) 09 06 24

15 Avenue Gambetta,
F-42300 Roanne;
tel. (77) 72 25 35

8 Avenue Denfert-Rochereau,
F-42000 St-Etienne;
tel. (77) 32 62 71

Aéroport de St-Etienne,
tel. (77) 32 62 71

40 rue Jean-Jaurès,
F-44600 St-Nazaire;
tel. (40) 22 20 37

6 rue George-Sand,
F-37000 Tours;
tel. (47) 61 12 28

Place de la Gare,   Hertz
32 rue Denis-Papin,
F-49000 Angers;
tel. (41) 88 07 53

4 Avenue Henri-Laudier,
F-18000 Bourges;
tel. (48) 70 22 92

6 Allée du Commandant-Charcot,
F-44000 Nantes;
tel. (40) 74 18 29

Aéroport de Nantes,
tel. (40) 75 15 55

Place de la Gare,
F-58000 Nevers;
tel. (86) 57 22 96

47 Avenue de Paris,
F-45000 Orléans;
tel. (38) 62 60 60

Esplanade Diderot,
F-42300 Roanne;
tel. (77) 72 44 19

4 Place Locarno,
F-42000 St-Etienne;
tel. (77) 32 22 25

Aéroport de St-Etienne,
tel. (77) 36 54 79

Rue du Commandant-L'Herminier,
F-44600 St-Nazaire;
tel. (40) 66 51 69

99 rue de Rouen,
F-49400 Saumur;
tel. (41) 38 25 33

Rue Fleming,
F-37000 Tours;
tel. (47) 61 02 54

InterRent

30 rue Denis-Papin,
F-49000 Angers;
tel. (41) 88 54 44

13 Quai de Versailles,
F-44000 Nantes;
tel. (40) 20 00 88

98–103 rue Bergson,
F-42000 St-Etienne;
tel. (77) 74 27 55

At railway stations

See Rail services

Coach tours

Many travel firms and agencies operate coach tours in the Loire valley, usually visiting the châteaux between Orléans and Angers, with a particular concentration in the area around Tours.

From Tours various local firms run half-day and day trips and visits to "Son et lumière" performances.

French Railways buses: see Rail services.

Services Touristiques de Touraine,
Bureau Circuits Châteaux de la Loire,
Gare SNCF,
F-37000 Tours;
tel. (47) 05 46 09

Information and reservations

Conducted visits

Most historic buildings other than churches, and also certain
parts of churches (the crypt, the treasury), can be seen only on
conducted tours. Since most visitors are French, English-
speaking guides are the exception rather than the rule, but
printed or duplicated leaflets in English are usually available.
The guide will expect a tip at the end of the tour.

At many sights visitors will find a *guide parlant* ("talking
guide"), a coin-operated device which gives a tape-recorded
commentary in French and sometimes also in other languages.

Tape-recorded guides

Cruising on rivers and canals

Holiday cruising on the canals and tributaries of the Loire has
become an increasingly popular activity in recent years.

The usual type of cruising boat is motor-driven, between 5.50
and 11 m (18 and 36 ft) in length and with between two and
six berths; normally no licence is required to "drive" them. They

Types of boat

Canal lock, Léré

are frequently equipped with a refrigerator, a galley, a toilet and heating.

A very recent variant is the so-called *carabarge*, an unsinkable pontoon, motor driven, with a "bridge" and space for a trailer caravan, making it a kind of house boat.

Boat hire firms

There are boat hire firms at Roanne, Decize, Nevers, Marseilles-lès-Aubigny, Angers and Nantes.

Information

Association des Voies Navigables de Bourgogne,
1–2 Quai de la République,
F-89000 Auxerre;
tel. (86) 52 26 27

Service Commun de Réservation du Bassin de la Maine,
Place du Président-Kennedy,
B.P. 2207,
F-49022 Angers Cedex;
tel. (41) 88 99 38

Comité de Promotion Touristique des Canaux Bretons
et des Voies Navigables de l'Ouest,
14 Boulevard Beaumont
F-35100 Rennes;
tel. (99) 79 36 26

Tourisme Accueil Loiret,
3 rue de la Bretonnerie,
F-45000 Orléans;
tel. (38) 62 04 88

Currency

The unit of currency is the French franc (F), which is made up of 100 centimes. There are banknotes for 10, 20, 50, 100 and 500 francs, and coins in denominations of 5, 10 and 20 centimes and $\frac{1}{2}$, 1, 2, 5 and 10 francs.

Rates of exchange
(February 1987)

1 F = 11.03p (UK)   £1 = 9.06 F
1 F = 16.39c (US) $1 = 6.10 F

Currency regulations

There are no restrictions on the import of either French or foreign currency.

The export of foreign currency in cash is permitted up to a value of 5000 F or to any higher amount which has been declared on entry into France. The export of French currency is subject to a limit of 5000 F.

It is advisable to take money in the form of traveller's cheques or Eurocheques or to have a Eurocheque card.

Many hotels and shops accept credit cards (Eurocard, Visa, Access, Diners Club, American Express, etc.).

Changing money

Currency can be changed in banks or official bureaux de change, but not in savings banks (*caisses d'épargne*). Banks are often closed on Mondays.

Girobank postcheques

If you have an account with the British Girobank you can cash "postcheques" for up to the equivalent of 600 F at French post offices.

Customs regulations

Personal effects and such things as camping and sports
equipment can be taken into France without formality. In
addition visitors are allowed the usual duty-free allowances of
alcohol and tobacco, etc. Visitors from Britain and other EEC
countries can take in 300 cigarettes or 150 cigarillos or 75
cigars or 400 grammes of tobacco, $1\frac{1}{2}$ litres of spirits over 38.8°
proof (22° Gay-Lussac) or 3 litres of alcoholic drinks not over
38.8° proof or 3 litres of fortified or sparkling wine, and 4 litres
of still table wine. For goods bought in a duty-free shop the
allowances are two-thirds of these amounts (250 grammes of
tobacco). The allowances of tobacco goods are doubled for
visitors from outside Europe.

For outboard motors of over 92 cc a *triptyque* or *carnet de
passages en douane* is required.

A deposit must be paid for the import of a portable television
set. It should be remembered, however, that British television
sets are incompatible with the French television system (see
Radio and television).

See Currency

Currency regulations

Diplomatic and consular offices

Embassy,
35 rue du Faubourg St-Honoré,
F-75008 Paris;
tel. (1) 2 66 91 42;
consular section tel. 2 60 33 06

United Kingdom

Consulate General,
105–9 rue du Faubourg St-Honoré,
F-75008 Paris;
tel. (1) 2 66 91 42

Consulate,
6 rue Lafayette,
F-44009 Nantes;
tel. (40) 48 57 47

Embassy,
2 Avenue Gabriel,
F-75008 Paris;
tel. (1) 2 96 12 02 and 2 61 80 75;
consular section tel. as for Embassy

United States of America

Embassy,
35 Avenue Montaigne,
F-75008 Paris;
tel. (1) 2 25 99 55

Canada

Consular Section,
4 rue Ventadour,
F-75001 Paris;
tel. (1) 0 73 15 83

Emergency calls

There are emergency telephones on all motorways and some *routes nationales*.

In towns of any size the Police de Secours can be called by dialling 17; in the country call the Gendarmerie. Motorists involved in a traffic accident must complete a *constat à l'amiable* before the vehicle is moved. If the vehicle has been seriously damaged an expert's examination is advised prior to the return to the UK. The *constat à l'amiable* was introduced by the French insurance companies and represents the "European Accident Statement Form". It must be signed by the other party, but if a dispute arises and one of the parties involved should refuse to complete the *constat à l'amiable* then the other party should immediately obtain a written report from a bailiff (*huissier*), which is known as a *constat d'huissier*. A bailiff can usually be found in any large town and charges a fee of 400 F for preparing the report. Normally the police are only called out to accidents where persons are injured, a driver is under the influence of alcohol or the accident impedes traffic flow. When attending an accident the police prepare a report known as a *procès verbal*.

After an accident the French authorities, at their discretion, may request a surety payment to cover the court costs or fines.

Breakdown service

If your car breaks down, endeavour to move it to the side of the road or to a position where it will obstruct the traffic flow as little as possible. If the car is fitted with hazard warning lights switch them on or, alternatively, place a warning triangle at the appropriate distance on the road behind the obstruction. If the vehicle breaks down on a motorway telephone the police (*Brigade de Gendarmerie*) from an emergency telephone or service station. The police will contact a garage for you, but should it be necessary to move the vehicle from the motorway for repair the choice of repair garage can be determined by the motorist. For breakdowns in Motorway Service/Motel or Filling Station areas the call for assistance must originate from the area to the police. On all other roads you are advised to seek local assistance as, at the time of going to press, there is no nationwide road assistance service in France.

Events

April	Bourges: Printemps de Bourges (a musical, folk and dramatic festival)
April–June	Orléans: Flower Show in the Parc de la Source
April–October	Amboise: Classical concerts in the church of St–Denis
May	Bourges: Old Town Festival Orléans: Jeanne d'Arc Festival Sancerre: Cheese Market Tours: Flower Parade
May–September	Châteaudun: Château concerts

Amboise: St John's Day (Midsummer)	25 June
Langeais: International Days of Music Tours: Musical Festival of Touraine	June–July
Loches: Marché Paysan (Country Fair) Sully-sur-Loire: Musical Festival	July
Orléans: Musical Summer Valençay: Festival of Music and Drama	July–August
Azay-le-Rideau: Summer concerts	July and September
Amboise: Wine Market Chinon: Medieval Market Langeais, Plessis-lès-Tours, Ussé: Summer concerts Sancerre: Wine Festival Tours: Summer concerts	August
Amboise: Summer concerts	September
St-Benoît-sur-Loire: Christmas midnight mass	December

Food and drink

French cuisine is world-famous both for quality and variety. Since the French have traditionally attached great importance to well-chosen and well-prepared food and are ready to devote ample time to a meal, eating and drinking are an important province of French life and the cuisine of France has become an element in its culture.

French cuisine

The best French cooking – *haute cuisine* – is characterised by the use of fresh vegetables and other ingredients and much butter and cream (*crème fraîche*). Herbs and spices are used on a considerable scale and in a variety of combinations. Famous, too, are the excellent French sauces.

In recent years there has been a great vogue for what is known as *nouvelle cuisine*, distinguished by less elaborate recipes and the use of the finest vegetables and other ingredients.

Alongside *haute cuisine* there is also the cuisine of the different provinces of France – *cuisine régionale* – which is likewise much esteemed by gourmets.

The commonest French drink is wine (see Wine). The wines of the Loire – for the most part light and refreshing – are drunk mainly in the area where they are grown.

Drinks

Beer is becoming increasingly popular. Most French beer is brewed in Alsace and in the N of the country.

The cider of Normandy, made from the local apples, is a refreshing drink. It may be either sweet (*doux*) or dry *(brut)*.

Colourless brandies are few in number. The favourite types are Cognac, Armagnac and Calvados, which is distilled from cider. For those who prefer soft drinks there are various mineral waters, fruit juices, lemonades, etc.

See Restaurants

Restaurants

Hotels

In general French hotels are good, reaching an excellent standard within their various categories. In a small town visitors are likely to be offered only a room with a *grand lit*, the broad French double bed, at a charge which is not much higher for two persons than for one. Most of the better hotels are approved and classified by the Commissariat Général au Tourisme as *hôtels de tourisme* and bear a sign to that effect. Detailed information about hotels can be obtained from the official "Guide des Hôtels de France", published annually, and the lists of hotels supplied free of charge by local Offices de Tourisme and Syndicats d'Initiative (see Information).

Many hotels in the various categories, particularly in areas where it is desired to promote tourism, have been modernised with the help of the Fédération Nationale des Logis de France, and these *logis de France* provide modern standards of comfort and amenity at moderate prices. Even more modestly priced are the *auberges rurales*, usually offering a family atmosphere and local country cooking. Booklets listing hotels in these two groups are issued annually.

Many hotels on main roads between towns are known as *relais* (the term applied to the old post-houses where travellers could change horses). These are usually of individual character and excellent quality; they may be listed, for example, as "Relais de Campagne et Châteaux-Hôtels" and "Relais du Silence".

The *relais routiers*, mostly used by long-distance drivers, lie on the main roads; they are usually more modest places but offering excellent value.

Hotel categories	French hotels are officially classified in five categories, ranging upwards from one to four stars and L, the luxury category.
Amboise	***Novotel Amboise, 17 rue des Sablonnières, 82 r. ***Chanteloup, 12 Route de Bléré, 25 r. ***Château de Pray, in Chargé, 16 r. **Belle-Vue, 12 Quai Charles-Guinot, 30 r. **Lion d'Or, 17 Quai Charles-Guinot, 23 r. **Parc, 8 rue Léonard-de-Vinci, 17 r.
Angers	***Mercure, Avenue Carnot, 86 r. ***Concorde, 18 Boulevard du Maréchal Foch, 73 r. ***d'Anjou, 1 Boulevard du Maréchal Foch, 51 r. ***Progrès, 26 rue Denis Papin, 41 r. **Lac de Maine, Route de Pruniers, 80 r. **de France, 8 Place de la Gare, 64 r. **de la Gare, 5 Place de la Gare, 55 r. **Univers, 2 Place de la Gare, 45 r. **Climat de France, rue du Chateau d'Orgemont, 42 r. **Royal Hôtel, 8 bis Place de la Visitation, 40 r. **Saint-Julien, 9 Place du Ralliement, 34 r. **de Champagne, 34 rue Denis Papin, 30 r.
Azay-le-Rideau	**Le Grand Monarque, Place de la République, 30 r. **Les Trois Lys, 2 rue du Château, 12 r. **Biencourt, 7 rue Balzac, 8 r.
La Baule	L****Hermitage, Esplanade du Casino, 230 r. L****Castel Marie-Louise, Esplanade du Casino, 31 r.

****Royal, Esplanade F.-André, 97 r.
***Majestic, Esplanade F.-André, 67 r.
***Alexandra, 3 Boulevard d'Armor, 40 r.
***Christina, 26 Boulevard Hennecart, 40 r.
***Les Pléiades, 28 Boulevard d'Armor, 40 r.
***Bellevue Plage, 27 Boulevard de l'Océan, 34 r.
***Alcyon, 19 Avenue des Pétrels, 32 r.
***Les Alizes, 10 Avenue de Rhuys, 32 r.
***Flepen, 145 Avenue de Lattre de Tassigny, 24 r.
***La Cantellerie, 10 Avenue de Saumur, 24 r.
**Des Dunes, 277 Avenue de Lattre de Tassigny, 44 r.
**Concorde, Avenue de la Concorde. 42 r.

****La Tonnellerie, 12 rue des Eaux-Bleues, 27 b.   **Beaugency**
**L'Ecu de Bretagne, Place du Martroi, 26 r.
**Sologne, 6 Place St-Firmin, 16 r.
**Relais des Templiers, 68 rue du Pont, 12 r.
*La Maille d'Or, 3 Avenue de Blois, 12 r.

***Novotel Blois, 20 rue des Pontières, 116 r.   **Blois**
**Grand Hôtel de Blois, 3 rue Porte-Côté, 50 r.
**du Château, 22 rue Porte-Côté, 47 r.
**Vendôme, 10 Avenue de Vendôme, 46 r.
**France et Guise, 3 rue Gallois, 45 r.
**Ibis, 15 rue de la Vallée-Maillard, 40 r.
**Gril Campanile, rue de la Vallée-Maillard, 39 r.
**Gare et Terminus, 8 Avenue Jean-Laigret, 33 r.
**Gerbe d'Or, 1 rue Bourg-Neuf, 25 r.
*Saint-Jacques, Place de la Gare, 32 r.
*Anne de Bretagne, 31 Avenue Jean-Laigret, 30 r.

***Central et d'Angleterre, 1 Place des Quatre-Piliers, 31 r.   **Bourges**
**Christina Hôtel, 5 rue de la Halle, 76 r.
**d'Artagnan, 19 Place Séraucourt, 71 r.
**Inter-Hotel Monitel, 73 rue Barbès, 48 r.
**Olympia, 66 Avenue d'Orléans, 42 r.
**de France, 4 Place Nirpied, 41 r.
**de la Poste, 22 rue Moyenne, 34 r.
**des Etrangers, 6 rue Cambournac, 32 r.
**Les Tilleuls, 7 Place de la Pyrotechnie, 29 r.

Grand Saint-Michel, in Bracieux, 38 r.   **Chambord

Bon Laboureur, Quai R. Mollot, 16 r.   **La Charité
**Grand Monarque, 33 Quai Clemenceau, 9 r.

Saint-Louis, 41 rue de la République, 42 r.   **Châteaudun
**de Beauce, 42 rue de Jallans, 23 r.
**Saint-Michel, 5 rue Péan, 18 r.
**Armorial, 59 rue Gambetta, 16 r.

***Hostellerie du Château, rue de-Lattre-de-Tassigny, 15 r.   **Chaumont**

***du Bon Laboureur et du Château, on the RN 76, 23 r.   **Chenonceaux**
***Ottoni, on the RN 76, 21 r.
**du Roy, 9 rue du Docteur-Bretonneau, 36 r.

Chris' Hotel, 12 Place Jeanne-d'Arc, 30 r.   **Chinon
**de France, 47 Place de l'Hôtel-de-Ville, 25 r.
**Diderot, 7 rue Diderot, 20 r.

**Boule d'Or, 66 Quai Jeanne-d'Arc, 19 r.
**Hostellerie Gargantua, 73 rue Voltaire, 13 r.
*du Progrès, 19 rue du Raineau, 16 r.

Cour-Cheverny

**des Trois Marchands, Place de l'Eglise, 44 r.
**Saint-Hubert, rue Nationale, 20 r.

Fontevraud-l'Abbaye

*Croix Blanche, 7 Place des Plantagenêts, 19 r.

Gien

**Sanotel, 21 Quai Sully, 48 r.
**Le Rivage, 1 Quai de Nice, 29 r.
*Terminus, Place de la Gare, 20 r.

Langeais

**La Duchesse Anne, 9 rue de Tours, 22 r.
**Hosten, 2 rue Gambetta, 14 r.

Loches

**Grand Hôtel de France, 6 rue Picois, 22 r.
**George Sand, 39 rue Quintefol, 18 r.
**Tour Saint-Antoine, 2 rue des Moulins, 18 r.
*Château, 18 rue du Château, 12 r.

Moulins

****de Paris, 21 rue de Paris, 29 r.
***Moderne, 9 Place Jean Moulin, 44 r.
**Grand Hôtel du Dauphin, 59 Place d'Allier, 62 r.
**Ibis, Route de Lyon, 43 r.
**Le Parc, 31 Avenue du Général-Leclerc, 26 r.
*Danguin et Terminus, Place de la Gare, 38 r.
*de l'Allier, 45 Place d'Allier, 30 r.

Nantes

L****Frantel, 3 rue du Dr-Zamenhof, 150 r.
L****Sofitel, rue A.-Millerand, 100 r.
***Mapotel Central, 4 rue du Couédic, 143 r.
***Vendée, 8 Allée Charcot, 90 r.
***de France, 24 rue Crébillon, 76 r.
***Astoria, 11 rue Richebourg, 45 r.
***Supotel, 9 rue d'Alger, 43 r.
***de Bourgogne, 9 Allée Charcot, 42 r.
***L'Hôtel, 6 Place de la Duchesse Anne, 31 r.
**Duchesse Anne, 3 Place de la Duchesse Anne, 75 r.
**Les Trois Marchands, 26 rue A.-Brossard, 64 r.
**de Paris, 2 rue Boileau, 58 r.
**Graslin, 1 rue Piron, 46 r.
**Grand Hôtel de Nantes, 2 rue Santeuil, 43 r.

Nevers

***PLM Loire, Quai de Médine, 60 r.
***Magdalena, Route de Paris, 38 r.
***Mapotel de Diane, 38 rue du Midi, 30 r.
**Moderne, 5 rue du Chemin-de-Fer, 40 r.
**La Folie, Route de Saulaies, 27 r.
**Terminus, 59 Avenue du Général-de-Gaulle, 25 r.
*de la Paix, 50 Avenue du Général-de-Gaulle, 34 r.
*Villa du Parc, 18 rue de Lourdes, 27 r.
*Blanc, 48 Avenue du Général-de-Gaulle, 22 r.

Noirmoutier

***Punta Lara, in La Guérinière, 78 r.
***Saint-Paul, in the Bois de la Chaize, 49 r.
***Général d'Elbée, in Noirmoutiers-en-l'Ile, 33 r.
**Beau Rivage, in the Bois de la Chaize, 30 r.
**Les Illettes, in Noirmoutier-en-l'Ile, 25 r.
**Fleur de Sel, in Les Coques, 23 r.
**Capucines, in Noirmoutier-en-l'ile, 21 r.

L****Sofitel, 44–46 Quai Barentin, 110 r.   **Orléans**
***Novotel, 2 rue Honoré-de- Balzac, 121 r.
***Terminus, 40 rue de la République, 47 r.
***Moderne, 37 rue de la République, 36 r.
***Les Cèdres, 17 rue du Maréchal-Foch, 32 r.
***Saint-Aignan, 3 Place Gambetta, 29 r.
**Arcade, 4 rue du Maréchal-Foch, 125 r.
**Gril Campanile, 326 rue Châteaubriand, 42 r.

Grand Hôtel de la Basilique, 18 rue de la Visitation, 70 r. **Paray-le-Monial
**Hostellerie des Trois Pigeons, 2 rue d'Argaud, 33 r.
**Terminus, 57 Avenue de la Gare, 22 r.

****Christel, 15 Boulevard Alexandre-Clair, 30 r. **Le Puy**
***Regina, 34 Boulevard du Maréchal-Fayolle, 38 r.
**Licorn, 25 Avenue Charles-Dupuy, 44 r.
**Cygne, 47 Boulevard du Maréchal-Fayolle, 41 r.
**Bristol, 7 Avenue du Maréchal-Foch, 35 r.
**Moulin de Barette, in Blavozy, 30 r.
**Val Vert, 6 Avenue Baptiste-Marcet, 23 r.
*de la Verveine, 6 Place Cadelade, 29 r.
*Lafayette, 17 Boulevard St-Louis, 24 r.

L**** Les Frères Troisgros, Place de la Gare, 24 r. **Roanne**
***Grand Hôtel, 18 Cours de la République, 45 r.
***Relais de Roanne, in St-Germain-l'Espinasse, 32 b.
**Terminus, 15 Cours de la République, 51 r.
**Ibis Roanne, Zone Industrielle de Coteau, 49 r.
**de France, 19 rue Alexandre-Roche, 42 r.

Labrador, 7 Place de l'Abbaye, 16 r. **St-Benoît-sur-Loire
*de la Madeleine, 65 rue Orléanaise, 12 r.

****Le Grand Hôtel, 10 Avenue de la Libération, 66 r. **St-Etienne**
***Frantel, rue de Wuppertal, 120 r.
***Novotel Saint-Etienne Aéroport, at the airport, 96 r.
***Terminus du Forez, 31 Avenue Denfert-Rochereau, 66 r.
***Astoria, Le Rond-Point, 33 r.
***Midi, 19 Boulevard Pasteur, 27 r.
**Des Arts, 11 rue Gambetta, 63 r.
**Hostellerie du Cheval Noir, 11 rue Francois Gillet, 45 r.
**Touring-Continental, 10, rue Francois Gillet, 25 r.
**Central Hôtel, 3 rue Blanqui, 25 r.

***du Berry, 1 Place de la Gare, 27 r. **St-Nazaire**
***Bon Acceuil, 39 rue Marceau, 13 r.
**Europe, 2 Avenue des Martyrs de la Résistance, 38 r.
**Bretagne, 7 Avenue de la République, 33 r.
**Terminus, 5 Avenue de la République, 24 r.
**Armoric, 92 Avenue de la République, 23 r.
**Dauphin, 33 rue Jean-Jaurès, 22 r.
**Belle Epee, 45 rue Jean Jaurès, 13 r.

Panoramic, Rempart des Augustins, 57 r. **Sancerre
**du Rempart, Rempart des Dames, 12 r.

***Budan, 3 Quai Carnot, 80 r. **Saumur**
**Terminus, 15 Avenue David d'Angers, 45 r.
**Gril Campanile, Côte de Bournan, 42 r.
**Les Moulins de Bournan, in Bagneux, 42 r.

      **du Roi René, 94 Avenue du Général-de-Gaulle, 37 r.
      **Hôtel de Londres, 48 rue d'Orléans, 26 r.
      *Central, 23 rue Daillé, 24 r.

Sully
      **de la Poste, 11 Faubourg St-Germain, 29 r.
      **du Pont de Sologne, 21 rue Porte-de-Sologne, 25 r.
      **Hostellerie Grand Sully, 10 Boulevard du Champ-de-Foire, 11 r.

Tours
      ****Méridien, 292 Avenue de Grammont, 125 r.
      ***de l'Univers, 5 Boulevard Heurteloup, 94 r.
      ***Grand Hôtel, 9 Place du Maréchal-Leclerc, 79 r.
      ***Bordeaux, 3 Place du Maréchal-Leclerc, 54 r.
      ***Central Hôtel, 21 rue Berthelot, 42 r.
      ***de France, 38–40 rue de Bordeaux, 35 r.
      ***Royal, 65 Avenue Grammont, 35 r.
      **Arcade, 1 rue Georges Claude, 139 r.
      **Terminus, 7–9 rue de Nantes, 54 r.
      **d'Armor, 26 bis Boulevard Heurteloup, 50 r.
      **de l'Europe, 12 Place du Maréchal-Leclerc, 50 r.
      **Ibis Tours Nord, Avenue André, 49 r.
      **Gambetta, 7 rue Gambetta, 39 r.
      **Criden, 65 Boulevard Heurteloup, 33 r.

Valençay
      ****d'Espagne, 9 rue du Château, 18 r.
      **Lion d'Or, Place du Marché, 15 r.

Vendôme
      **Saint-Georges, rue de la Poterie, 37 r.
      **Vendôme, 15 Faubourg Chartrain, 20 r.
      *Château, Place du Château, 20 r.
      *Saint-Michel, 31 Mail du Général-Leclerc, 18 r.
      *Moderne, 8 Boulevard Tremault, 16 r.

Villandry
      **Cheval Rouge, in Joué-lès-Tours, 20 r.

Information

Secrétariat d'Etat au Tourisme	Secrétariat d'Etat au Tourisme, 8 Avenue de l'Opera, F-75041 Paris Cedex 01; tel. (1) 7 66 51 35
United Kingdom	French Government Tourist Office, 178 Piccadilly, London W1V 0AL; tel. (01) 493 3171
United States	French Government Tourist Office, 610 Fifth Avenue, New York, NY 10021; tel. (212) 757 1125
	645 N. Michigan Avenue, Suite 430, Chicago, IL 60601; tel. (312) 337 6301
	9401 Wilshire Boulevard, Beverly Hills, CA 90112; tel. (213) 271 6665 and 272 2661

360 Post Street,
San Francisco;
tel. (415) 986 4161

20 Queen Street West,   **Canada**
Toronto;
tel. (416) 593 4717

1840 Sherbrooke Street West,
Montreal H3H 2W9;
tel. (514) 931 3855

Office de Tourisme,   **Amboise**
Quai du Général-de-Gaulle,
F-37402 Amboise;
tel. (47) 57 09 28

Office de Tourisme   **Angers**
(closed Sundays in winter),
Place de la Gare,
F-49000 Angers;
tel. (41) 87 72 50

Syndicat d'Initiative   **Azay-le-Rideau**
(closed Sunday),
Rue Gambetta (summer),
Mairie (winter),
F-37190 Azay-le-Rideau;
tel. (47) 43 34 40 (summer),
43 32 11 (winter)

Office de Tourisme,   **La Baule**
Place de la Victoire,
F-44504 La Baule;
tel. (40) 24 34 44

Office de Tourisme,   **Beaugency**
28 Place du Martroi,
F-45190 Beaugency;
tel. (38) 44 54 42

Office du Tourisme,   **Blois**
Pavillion Anne de Bretagne,
3 Avenue Jean-Laigret,
F-41000 Blois;
tel. (54) 74 06 49

Office de Tourisme,   **Bourges**
Rue Moyenne,
F-18000 Bourges;
tel. (48) 24 75 33

Syndicat d'Initiative,   **La Charité**
49 Grande Rue (summer),
Mairie (winter),
F-58400 La Charité-sur-Loire;
tel. (86) 70 16 12

Office de Tourisme,   **Châteaudun**
3 rue Toufaire,
F-28200 Châteaudun;
tel. (37) 45 22 46

Practical Information

Chenonceaux	Syndicat d'Initiative, 1 bis rue du Château, F-37150 Chenonceaux; tel. (47) 29 94 45
Chinon	Office de Tourisme, 12 rue Voltaire, F-37500 Chinon; tel. (47) 93 17 85
Gien	Office du Tourisme, Pavillon Touristique, Rue Anne-de-Beaujeu, F-45500 Gien; tel. (38) 67 25 28
Langeais	Syndicat d'Initiative, Mairie, F-37130 Langeais; tel. (47) 96 58 22
Loches	Office du Tourisme, Place de la Marne, F-37600 Loches; tel. (47) 59 07 98
Moulins	Office de Tourisme, Place de l'Hôtel-de-Ville, F-03000 Moulins; tel. (70) 44 14 14
Nantes	Office du Tourisme, Place du Change, F-44000 Nantes; tel. (40) 47 04 51
Nevers	Office municipal du Tourisme, 31 rue du Rempart, F-58000 Nevers; tel. (86) 58 07 03
Noirmoutier	Syndicat d'Initiative, Rue du Pont, F-85330 Noirmoutier-en-l'Ile; tel. (51) 39 80 71
Orléans	Office du Tourisme, Place Albert-Ier, F-45000 Orléans; tel. (38) 53 05 95
Paray-le-Monial	Office du Tourisme, Place de la Poste, F-71600 Paray-le-Monial; tel. (85) 81 10 92
Le Puy	Office de Tourisme, Place du Breuil, F-43000 Le Puy; tel. (71) 09 38 41

Office du Tourisme, Cours de la République, F-42300 Roanne; tel. (77) 71 51 77	**Roanne**
Office d'Accueil et d'Information, 12 rue Gérentet, F-42000 St-Etienne; tel. (77) 25 12 14	**St-Etienne**
Syndicat d'Initiative, Place François-Blancho, F-44600 St-Nazaire; tel. (40) 22 40 65	**St-Nazaire**
Syndicat d'Initiative, Mairie, F-18300 Sancerre; tel. (36) 54 00 26	**Sancerre**
Office du Tourisme, 25 rue Beaurepaire, F-49400 Saumur; tel. (41) 51 03 06	**Saumur**
Syndicat d'Initiative, Place du Général-de-Gaulle, F-45600 Sully-sur-Loire; tel. (38) 35 32 21	**Sully**
Office de Tourisme, Place de la Gare, F-37000 Tours; tel. (47) 05 58 08	**Tours**
Syndicat d'Initiative, Avenue de la Résistance, F-36600 Valençay; tel. (54) 00 04 42	**Valençay**
Office de Tourisme, 45 rue de la Poterie, F-41100 Vendôme; tel. (54) 77 05 07	**Vendôme**

Maps and plans

Visitors who want to get off the main traffic routes will find it useful to have more detailed maps than the general map accompanying this Guide. The following is a selection.

Michelin detailed maps of France. The sheets required for the area covered by this Guide are 60, 63, 64, 65, 67, 68, 69, 73 and 76.

1:200,000

IGN map.

1:250,000 and 1:100,000

Motoring in France

	In France, as in the rest of continental Europe, traffic travels on the right, with overtaking on the left. Safety belts must be worn.
Priority including Roundabouts	The general rule is to give way to traffic entering a junction from the right, although this varies at roundabouts (see below). This is one aspect of driving in France which may cause the British driver the most confusion because his whole training and experience makes it unnatural. Road signs indicate priority or loss of priority and tourists are well advised to make sure that they understand such signs.

In built-up areas drivers must slow down and be prepared to stop at all road junctions. If there are no priority signs give way to traffic from the right. All important roads outside built-up areas have right of way called *Passage protégé* signified by signs.

Visiting motorists should be extra careful when negotiating roundabouts as new priorities have been introduced. At unsigned roundabouts traffic entering has priority; at signed roundabouts bearing the words *Vous n'avez pas la priorité* or *Cédez le passage* traffic on the roundabout has priority.

In built-up areas with adequate street lighting sidelights must be used after dark. At night warning signals must be given by flashing the headlights, not by the use of the horn.

Foreign vehicles are not required to use the yellow headlights which are normal in France. If you have a right-hand-drive car and expect to be driving at night it is advisable to adjust the dipping arrangements. It is compulsory for visiting motorists to equip their vehicle with a set of replacement bulbs.

Speed limits	Maximum permitted speeds: on toll motorways 130 km/h (80 m.p.h.) on expressways 110 km/h (68 m.p.h.) on other roads 90 km/h (56 m.p.h.) in built-up areas 60 km/h (37 m.p.h.)

In rainy conditions the limits are reduced from 130 to 110 km/h (68 m.p.h.) and from 110 to 100 km/h (62 m.p.h.) and from 90 to 80 km/h (49 m.p.h.).
Drivers who have held a full driving licence for less than a year are restricted to a speed of 90 km/h (55 m.p.h.).

Parking regulations	See Parking

Opening times

Shopping centres	Shopping centres (*centres commerciaux*), usually situated on the outskirts of large towns, are normally open on weekdays (including Saturdays) from 9 a.m. to 7 p.m. (sometimes to 9 p.m.).
Other shops Foodshops	The opening times for smaller establishments are less strictly regulated. Foodshops and bakeries open early in the morning, and are usually open for at least part of the day on Sundays and public holidays. Most shops have a lunch break from noon to 2 or 3 p.m.

Many museums, châteaux and other tourist sights, and some churches are closed at lunchtime. During the main holiday season there are a few exceptions to this rule.
Visitors should not, of course, look round churches during services.

Museums, châteaux, etc.

Parking

At most of the main tourist sights there is adequate parking space (usually on payment; sometimes guarded).

Many towns have a *zone bleue* ("blue zone"), indicated by signs and road markings, within which parked cars must display a parking disc (*disque*) which allows parking for a limited time. Discs can be obtained from the police or from motoring organisations.
There is no general ban on parking on the left-hand side of a road or street. Many towns have a system of *stationnement alterné* under which the side on which parking is permitted alternates daily or half-monthly. Parking is prohibited on yellow lines.

"Zone bleue"

A recent development in French towns is a "pay and display" system of parking in which tickets obtained from machines (*horodateurs*), the cost varying according to the time required, must be displayed behind the car's windscreen.

"Pay and display"

Postal and telephone services

Post offices are open Monday to Friday 8 a.m.–noon and 2–6 p.m. Saturday 8 a.m.–noon.

The easiest way of telephoning, both within France and abroad, is to use one of the coin-operated telephones to be found everywhere.

Telephoning

United Kingdom to France: 010 33
France to the United Kingdom: 19 44

International dialling codes

United States to France: 011 33
France to the United States: 19 1

Canada to France: 011 33
France to Canada: 19 1

When dialling from France to Britain the zero prefixed to the local dialling code should be omitted.

Public holidays

1 January (New Year's Day)
Easter Monday
1 May (Labour Day)
Ascension

Whit Monday
14 July (National Day: taking of the Bastille, 1789)
15 August (Assumption)
1 November (All Saints)
11 November (Armistice Day)
25 December

Radio and television

Radio

British radio programmes can be received in France on long and medium waves as well as on short waves (BBC World Service).

Messages for tourists

In cases of great emergency the BBC (tel. 01–580 4468) will accept messages, from near relations only, which will be broadcast on Radio France Inter (long wave, 1829 metres).

Television

Since television transmitters have a relatively short range, it is not usually possible to receive British television programmes in France, except in areas near Britain.
Since French television uses a different system, British portable television sets cannot receive French programmes.

Rail services

The nationalised French Railways (Sociéte Nationale des Chemins de Fer Français, SNCF) maintain a high standard of comfort and efficiency. The main lines are served by numerous TEE trains (Trans-Europe Expresses), long-distance trains and expresses (*rapides*).
Since 1981 France has had the world's fastest train, the TGV (Train à Grande Vitesse), running between Paris and Lyons at speeds of up to 260 km/h (160 m.p.h.).
Since the main lines radiate from Paris, the route described in this Guide (p. 28) cannot be followed all the way by rail. There is a line from Le Puy to Gien and another from Orléans to Nantes and St-Nazaire.
The French Railways run a number of services of interest to tourists.

Train + Auto

Under arrangements made by French Railways with a car hire firm visitors can have a hired car waiting for them at certain French railway systems: the package is known as "Train + Auto". Stations where this service is available include, within the area covered by this Guide, Angers, Blois, Bourges, Moulins, Nantes, Nevers, Orléans, Le Puy, Roanne, St Etienne, St-Nazaire, Saumur and Tours.

Train + Vélo

Rail travellers can hire bicycles at many French railway stations, under the arrangement known as "Train + Vélo", which is available at Amboise, La Baule, Beaugency, Blois, Chinon, Langeais, Loches, Nevers, Orléans, St-Nazaire, Saumur, Tours and Vendôme.

Coach tours

Regular sightseeing coach tours are run from Angers, La Baule, and Tours.

French Railways,
179 Piccadilly,
London W1V 0BA;
tel. (01) 493 4451.

Information

Restaurants

In France even restaurants of unpretentious aspect in the country may well offer a menu of considerable quality. It will often be worth while to discuss the choice of dishes with the owner of the restaurant, the *patron* or *patronne*. When eating à la carte it is well to keep an eye on prices, for with a wide choice of dishes to select from the cost can mount up. For the quality of food offered, however, prices are generally not unreasonable. It is common practice to offer fixed-price tourist menus which are excellent value.

See Hotels

Restaurants in hotels

The following is merely a selection of the larger restaurants.

Auberge du Mail, 32 Quai du Général-de-Gaulle
Monseigneur, 12 Quai Charles-Guinot

Amboise

Le Logis, 17 rue St-Laud
Le Quéré, 9 Place du Ralliement
Le Toussaint, 7 rue Toussaint

Angers

Le Vert d'eau, 9 Boulevard G. Dumesnil
Le Muscadin, 10 rue A.-Riché

Azay-le-Rideau

L'Espadon, 2 Avenue de la Plage
Henri, 161 Avenue de-Lattre-de-Tassigny
Chalet Suisse, 114 Avenue du Général-de-Gaulle
Voile d'Or, in Le Pouliguen, Avenue de la Plage

La Baule

Hostellerie de la Loire, 8 rue de-Lattre-de-Tassigny
La Péniche, Promenade du Mail
Noë, 10 bis Avenue de Vendôme
L'Epoque, in Ménars

Blois

Jacques Cœur, 3 Place Jacques-Cœur
Auberge du Val d'Auron, 170 rue Lazenay
Ile d'Or, 39 Boulevard Juranville

Bourges

A la Bonne Foi, 91 rue C.-Barrière

La Charité

Caveau des Fouleurs, 33 rue des Fouleries
La Rose, 12 rue Lambert-Licors

Châteaudun

Au Gâteau Breton

Chenonceaux

Au Plaisir Gourmand, 2 rue Parmentier
Boule d'Or, 66 Quai Jeanne-d'Arc

Chinon

La Licorne, Rue R.-d'Arbrissel

Fontevraud-l'Abbaye

Beau Site et La Poularde, 13 Quai de Nice

Gien

153

Practical Information

Moulins	Restaurant des Cours, 36 Cours Jean-Jaurès Jacquemart, 10 Place de l'Hôtel-de-Ville
Nantes	L'Esquinade, 7 rue St-Denis Coq Hardi, 22 Allée du Commandant-Charcot Le Palatium, Place Aristide-Briand Les Maraîchers, 21 rue Fouré Auberge du Château, 5 Place de la Duchesse-Anne Le Nantais, 161 rue Hauts-Pavés
Nevers	Auberge de la Porte du Croux, 17 rue de la Porte-du-Croux Auberge Ste-Marie, 25 rue Mouesse La Renaissance, in Magny-Cours
Noirmoutier	La Marée, in Noirmoutier-en-l'Ile
Orléans	La Crémaillère, 34 rue Notre-Dame-de-Recouvrance La Poutrière, 8 rue Brèche Le Bigorneau, 54 rue des Turcies Auberge de la Montespan, in St-Jean-de-la-Ruelle Les Antiquaires, 222 rue de Bourgogne
Paray-le-Monial	Aux Vendanges de Bourgogne, 5 rue Denis-Papin
Le Puy	Sarda, 12 rue Chênebouterie Hostellerie de la Poste, 53 Boulevard St-Louis
Roanne	Auberge Costelloise, 2 Avenue de la Libération Ferme Napoléon, in Lentigny
St-Etienne	Pierre Gagnaire, 3 rue Georges-Teissier Le Bouchon, 7 rue Robert Le Chantecler, 5 Cours Fauriel
St-Nazaire	Au Bon Accueil, 39 rue Marceau
Sancerre	Auberge Alphonse Mellot, 16 Place de la Halle La Tasse d'Argent, 18 Rempart des Augustins
Saumur	Gambetta, 12 rue Gambetta
Sully	Hostellerie Grand Sully, Boulevard du Champ-de-Foire Esplanade, Place Pilier
Tours	Barrier, 101 Avenue de la Tranchée Le Lyonnais, 48 rue Nationale La Rôtisserie Tourangelle, 23 rue du Commerce Les Tuffeaux, 19 rue Lavoisier La Petite Marmite, 103 Avenue de la Tranchée La Poivrière, 13 rue du Change Au Gué de Louis XI, 36 Quai de la Loire Bistro 17, 17 Place de la Victoire
Valençay	Au Chêne Vert
Vendôme	Le Paris, 1 rue Darreau Le Daumier, 17 Place de la République
Villandry	Le Cheval Rouge

Roads

France has a dense network of roads, and even minor roads are usually in good condition.

The motorways (*autoroutes*) which have been constructed in recent years will have a total length of some 6216 km/3862 miles by the end of 1984. Except on some short sections round large cities tolls (*péage*) are payable. In the region covered by this Guide the motorways are, in general, useful only as a means of reaching the general area.

Motorways

The bulk of traffic, however, is still carried by France's excellent system of national highways (*routes nationales*). These have red and white kilometre stones bearing the number of the road (e.g. N555), and frequently have only three lanes, the central lane being used for overtaking in both directions. The total road network is so extensive that traffic is usually relatively light – though there may be hold-ups during the holiday season on the roads radiating from Paris.

Routes nationales

The *routes départementales* are less important roads, marked by yellow and white kilometre stones with the road number (e.g. D555).
In recent years many *routes nationales* have become *routes départementales*, usually with a slight alteration in the number.

Routes départementales

Son et lumière

During the summer "Son et lumière" ("Sound and light") shows are put on after dark at sites of particular tourist interest, particularly châteaux. These involve dramatic presentations of historic episodes, with impressive lighting effects, which often take in not only the building itself but the surrounding gardens or park as well. Increasingly, too, plays are performed in these theatrical settings.
In some places, however, these performances have been restricted on grounds of cost.
Places where *Son et lumière* shows can be seen include Amboise, Azay-le-Rideau, Beaugency, Blois, Chambord, Chenonceau, Chinon, Cour-Cheverny and Valençay.

Time

France observes Central European Time, one hour ahead of Greenwich Mean Time. During Summer Time, from the end of March to the end of September, clocks are advanced an hour.

Tipping

Tipping practice in France ("tip" = *pourboire*) is much the same as in other European countries. Guides in châteaux, museums, etc., expect to receive a tip, as do the attendants who

Son et lumière at Chinon

show people to their seats in theatres and cinemas, as well as lock-keepers on canals.

Bills for meals in restaurants and drinks in cafés usually include a service charge.

Travel documents

Visitors from Britain and most western countries require only a valid passport (or British Visitor's Passport) to enter France; nationals of many western European countries require only an identity card.

National driving licences and car registration documents are accepted in France, and should always be carried when driving. The minimum age at which a visitor may drive a temporarily imported car or motorcycle (over 80 cc) is 18 years. Although nationals of EEC countries are not required to have an international insurance certificate ("green card"), it is desirable to have one, since otherwise only third-party cover is provided. Foreign vehicles must carry an oval nationality plate.

Health insurance cover is available to EEC nationals on the same basis as for French citizens (insured persons and pensioners). For this purpose British visitors should obtain a certificate of entitlement (form E111) from their local Social Security office. It is desirable also to take out a supplementary short-term insurance.

Water sports

The scope for boating on the Loire itself is limited, given the considerable variations in water level. Canoeing enthusiasts, however, may find opportunities of practising their sport.
Conditions are more favourable on the artificial lakes formed by the dams on the Loire to the N of Le Puy, where there are opportunities for rowing (boat hire at many places), sailing and wind-surfing. There are also excellent conditions for water sports on the Vendée coast, though here regard must be had to the tides.

See Cruising on rivers and canals   Cruising

When to go

On the highest stretches of the Loire it can still be quite cool in May. Downstream from Le Puy the best months are May, June, September and the first half of October.
In summer, during the school holidays in France and the neighbouring countries, there are very large numbers of visitors, particularly in the château area, and this may lead to difficulty in finding accommodation.

Wine

The Loire valley is one of France's most northerly wine-producing regions. In view of the considerable climatic and geological differences along the course of the river the character of the wines varies from area to area; but in general it can be said that the Loire wines are light and dry, and are mostly drunk in and around the area of production. On the lower Loire, particularly around Saumur, sparkling wine is made in some quantity.
Farthest upstream are the vineyards of Sancerre and Pouilly, producing dry white wines which go very well with fish but on the whole do not improve with age.
Touraine has such well-known wine towns as Vouvray. Here, too, white wine predominates; in addition to dry wines there are also sweet and semi-sweet types, which keep well.
The only considerable red-wine area on the Loire is around Chinon. The red and rosé wines of Chinon and Bourgueil are fresh and fruity.
S of Saumur and Angers are the vineyards of Anjou, which, in addition to other types, produce highly aromatic dessert wines.
At the western end of the Loire valley, around Nantes, the predominant wine is Muscadet, which was long in achieving recognition outside its home area. Muscadet (not to be confused with Muscat, an aromatic and sweetish muscatel wine which is not produced in the Loire valley) is light, fresh and very dry – the ideal accompaniment to the seafood of the Atlantic coastal region.

A vineyard near Sancerre

Youth hostels

France has more than 300 youth hostels (*auberges de jeunesse*), which can be used by foreign visitors with an international youth hostel card (obtainable from the youth hostels organisation in their own country). Advance booking is advisable in July and August; the maximum stay permitted is usually three nights.

Within the area covered by this Guide, there are youth hostels at Beaugency, Blois, Bourges, Châteaudun, Orléans, Roanne, St-Etienne, Saumur and Tours.

Information

Fédération Unie des Auberges de Jeunesse,
6 rue Mesnil,
F-75116 Paris;
tel. (1) 2 61 84 03

Index